The Anstruther Reader

The Anstruther Reader

Ten Years of Poems

Broadsides

and Manifestos

Edited by Jim Johnstone

Introduction copyright © Jim Johnstone 2024
Copyright © is retained by the individual authors 2024

Edited by Jim Johnstone
Cover design by Erica Smith
Typeset by Erica Smith

Palimpsest Press would like to thank the Canada Council for the Arts, and the Ontario Arts Council for their support of our publishing program. We also acknowledge the assistance of the Government of Ontario through the Ontario Book Publishing Tax Credit.

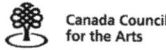 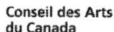  

Library and Archives Canada Cataloguing in Publication

Title: The Anstruther reader / edited by Jim Johnstone.
Names: Johnstone, Jim, 1978- editor

Identifiers: Canadiana (print) 20240430654 | Canadiana (ebook) 20240431987
ISBN 9781990293832 (softcover) | ISBN 9781990293849 (EPUB)

Subjects: LCSH: Canadian poetry—21st century.
CSH: Canadian poetry (English)—21st century. | LCGFT: Poetry.

Classification: LCC PS8293.1 .A67 2024 | DDC C811/.608—dc23

Printed and Bound in Canada

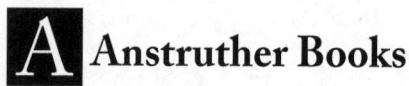

Contents

Introduction 13

Black Ash 23

Klara du Plessis — *Wax Lyrical*

The pragmatism of a girl entering a room 25
Wax lyrical 26
Dream in radical disclosure 29

Bardia Sinaee — *Blue Night Express*

Wireless Fidelity 31
Sonnet 32
The Weather 33

Allison LaSorda — *Playdate*

Coven 34
Playdate 35
Fish & Bird 36

T. Liem — *Tell Everybody I Say Hi*

At the museum without you 37
Everything I do is political 38
Work 39

Shazia Hafiz Ramji — *Prosopopoeia*

Sense 40
An Ambulance Speaks to Coyotes 41
Fundamentally Caring 42

Emily Skov-Nielsen — *Volta*

Volta 43
Menstromania 45

Contents

R.P. LaRose — *A Dream in the Bush*

Under the Snow 47
A Dream in the Bush While Living on Fish 49
Some Words Held in a Love Poem 50

David Ly — *Stubble Burn*

Stubble Burn 51
I Just Wanted a Blue Hawaiian 53
White+++ 54

Lily Wang — *Everyone in Your Dream is You*

In Hope 55
Mood Ring 56
To Recap: 57

Fawn Parker — *Weak Spot*

Golden Rays of Chemo 58
Strawberry Thief 59
In the Gift Shop 62

Oubah Osman — *Hereditary Blue*

Horner Hybridity 63
Drop 64
Hereditary Blue 65

Manahil Bandukwala — *Paper Doll*

Rosewater 66
To Be Important 67
I can't shelve my race to study for a midterm 68

Jaclyn Desforges — *Hello Nice Man*

Lacuna 69
In Which an Incel Steps on a Snail 70
Home Address 72

Contents

Jason Purcell — *A Place More Hospitable*
    The Spore Collector 73
    Bird House 74
    Men in the Gut 75

Tolu Oloruntoba — *Manubrium*
    If Tildes Approximate Wings for the Barrel I'm In 76
    In Which I, Again, am Fighting My Way Out of Things 77
    She Says— 78

Terese Mason Pierre — *Surface Area*
    Treatment 80
    Lines 82

Alison Braid-Fernandez — *Little Hunches*
    On Some Good Days 83
    Letter to Anne from Kitsilano 84
    Asturias 85

Mahaila Smith — *Claw Machine*
    Sappho 86
    Let Go 87
    Flick Off! 88

Benjamin C. Dugdale — *Saint Rat O'Sphere's Formica Canticle Poems*
    Imperial Cirrus Distortion 90
    Night Herding Song 91
    R a t t e r r a t t a n 93

Amanda Merpaw — *Put the Ghosts Down Between Us*
    Transmigration 95
    Rhizomatic Thinking 96
    The Communist's Daughter 98

Contents

Patrick Grace — *Dastardly*
Trespass 101
Dastardly 102
It's Like That, Is It 103

Joseph Kidney — *Terra Firma, Pharma Sea*
A Ghost of Him that Lets Me 104
Mori Point 105
Yanko Adrift 106

Shawn Adrian — *Metanoia's Prairie*
Near the Garden (of Eden) 108
Dandelion Reverie 109
Addendum: (Sin) 110

Melissa Schnarr — *Secondhand Moccasins*
Northern Lights 111
Displace 113
This is not a discovery 115

Emma Rhodes — *Razor Burn*
My Queer 117
Here and everywhere, I miss you 120

Pin Oak 123

Cassidy McFadzean
On Wearing the Leggings of Earthly Delights 125

David Barrick
This Sudden Night Walk Holds Everything 127

Katie Fewster-Yan
Gull 128

Contents

Shane Neilson
Be With Us in Our Sadness 129

Michael Prior
Palinode 131

Conor Mc Donnell — *The Book of Retaliations*
mordant 133
ho m I? 134
from tiny beginning 135

Mark Laliberte — *asemanticasymmetry*
Improbable Box 136
Ladder 137
Sigil 138

Gary Barwin — *The Human Body*
Hearing – The Ear 139
Accommodation 140
Sensation 141

Daze Jefferies — *water/wept*
fragments, *water/wept* 142

Christopher Patton — *Inanna Scient*
from *Inanna Scient* 146

Hemlock 151

M. Travis Lane — *Truth or Beauty* 153
John Nyman — *Slogan, Substance, Dream* 158
Dani Spinosa — *Visual Poetry for Women* 162
Yusra Usmani — *Poetry as Spectacle* 168
Robert Colman — *Perfectly Imperfect* 174

Contents

White Pine 179

James Lindsay — *Ekphrasis! Ekphrasis!*
    How Does It Feel 181
    Double Self-Portrait 182

Virginia Konchan — *The New Alphabets*
    Name me transient 183
    Here is your face 184
    The new alphabets 185

Kirby — *What Do You Want to Be Called?*
    "Can David Come Out to Play?" 186
    Kindness 188

Ayaz Pirani — *Bachelor of Art*
    Nakalanki 189
    Ali's Tiger 190
    Gardener 192

Chris Hutchinson — *Meanwhile, Myrmidons*
    What I Want Isn't What I Want to Want 193
    Creation 194
    Home & Garden 195

Marc di Saverio — *Aftersongs*
    The Man with the Microchip in His Right Hand 196
    Standing on Opposite Sides of the Stream 197
    Sonnet of Impending Ending 198

Lisa Martin — *Typology*
    ENFJ 199
    INFJ 200
    INTJ 201

Contents

Matthew Walsh — *ICQ*
    Bliss 202
    Soft Core 203
    Iamb 204

Khashayar "Kess" Mohammadi — *The Divine Bergamot*
    Ghazal 14 205
    Ghazal 441 206

Simina Banu — *harmony in Beach Foam*
    from *harmony in Beach Foam* 208

Blair Trewartha — *Human Energy*
    Half-Earth 212
    Modern American Worship 213

Triny Finlay — *Anxious Attachment Style*
    Livewire 214
    We Cannot Be Contained 216

Darren Bifford — *Some Trivial Reason*
    Purgatory 217
    Paradise 219

Sarah Burgoyne — *Air's Error*
    Instructions for Recognition 222

Matt Rader — *Atmospheric Moon River*
    Atmospheric Moon River 228

Angela Hibbs — *Sky*
    Power 233
    Plot Points 234
    The Ocean's Bookie 235

Contents

Janette Platana — *New Fairious*
    The Literacy Fairy 236
    The Fairies Reify & Deify 237
    The Second Coming of The Yeats Fairy 238

Douglas Walbourne-Gough — *Colour Work*
    Orange 239
    Red 240
    Purple 241

Jenna Lyn Albert — *mal à l'aise*
    mal à l'aise 242
    floriography I 243
    so who does what during, you know? 244

MICHAEL CHANG — *SWEET MOSS*
    SPECIAL SNOOZE 245
    LOW-KEY HIT OF THE SUMMER 246

Anstruther Checklist 249

Biographies 257

About the Editor 269

Introduction

Balance is different here. The air, too. Inside of a mountain hollowed out. Then diesel. The sound of a chainsaw lowered into water. Up, a spray of green. Down, a pitch black eye. Half a mile out, leaves blur over the lakebed, beachfront. Leaves becoming needles—pointillist fingers of white pine. Each wave split on the bow is a step toward veins of igneous rock, the sixty-foot hemlocks that tower over the lake. Chainsaw an outboard motor. Motor cut before a black dock (unseen unless you know it's there) becomes a path emptying into the forest. Balance restored.

Every summer, I travel to a cabin on the western shore of Anstruther Lake, making the final leg of the journey by boat since the location can only be reached by water. I often cross the lake with poets—both physically and in book form—the latter including Earle Birney, my foremost influence as a young writer, and Christopher Dewdney, who's written extensively about the natural history of Southern Ontario, detailing the rock formations that constitute the Canadian Shield. Dewdney's fossilized rocks underpin the Kawartha Lakes, and his "primordial atmosphere" is invariably the first thing I notice when I arrive. Place is a living materialization on Anstruther Lake, where the landscape gives off a "kind of memory vapour."

Introduction

That landscape is what urged my wife, Erica, and I to name our nascent press after the lake in 2014. Married a year, we spent much of the summer at Anstruther perched on a stony beach reading poems and taking photographs, several of which were shot through water. One particular image, taken of the lakebed in black and white, mysteriously flared with the light of the night sky as if the cosmos had been transposed on Anstruther's metamorphic foundation. Erica and I felt the photograph had the qualities of a visual poem, and it became a sort of creative omphalos. We paired it with poems written by Shane Neilson, its monochromatic nebulas blazing on the cover of *We Need Our Names*.

Along with Jess Taylor's *Never Stop*, we released *We Need Our Names* to inaugurate the founding of Anstruther Press. Because I was a bookmaker with very little experience, the early Anstruther titles looked similar to the books I'd published at Devon Gallant's Cactus Press between 2008 and 2012, featuring crudely designed, inky covers often stamped with handmade art. *We Need Our Names* and *Never Stop* were envisioned and produced in this spirit, before Anstruther Press had a logo or a masthead. Still, even if they look like Cactus Press productions, these chapbooks were an important first step, announcing our intention to build an evolving, print-based poetic community.

Balance, difference

Over the past ten years—balance uneven, diesel burning over water—Anstruther Press has been shaped by my wife's artistry. Putting her energy into the production and design elements of the press, Erica adds professionalism to the enterprise that I couldn't have realized on my own. The truth's there in the "A" logo carved out of Anstruther Lake's waves; it's there in the singular covers on the book table at seasonal launches; and it's there in Erica's exhortation that we select projects with an eye towards pairing emerging and established poets to cross-pollinate and bring added attention to first-time authors. In a forest of hemlock and white pine, there's always room for discovery, the moment when the black ash and birch trees that weren't seen at a distance become clear to the observers in a boat approaching the shore.

The same mandate shapes *The Anstruther Reader*, which begins with debut chapbooks, then moves to include broadsides, vispo, manifestos, and chapbooks

Jim Johnstone

by poets who have already published trade collections. Of all of our books, it's the debuts that I'm most passionate about, giving new authors a chance to have their work vetted, edited, and branded at the micropress level. My own story began this way at Surly Editions, established by Dani Couture to publish my now extinct chapbook *Siamese Poems*. I've documented this experience elsewhere, but it bears repeating that Dani's editorial care—which included handwritten feedback as well as detailed conversations about poetic craft—shaped my belief that mentorship should be a foundational principle of any publishing operation.

Of course, vetting manuscripts and offering critical feedback to authors leaves publishers open to questions of intention. In an article on gatekeeping in *Medium*, Rebecca Roach contends that: "The way we publish poems privileges the publication over the artist and reader. The system is exclusive, political, homogenous—almost, by definition, unable to accommodate variety accurately or fairly." To combat this kind of bias, Erica and I decided to form an editorial board to bring multiple voices to the fore when selecting and preparing books for publication. Because Anstruther Press aims to publish authors from across Canada, the editorial board is spread out geographically, with the current incarnation spanning from British Columbia (David Ly) to Ontario (Amanda Merpaw, Blair Trewartha, and Daniel Scott Tysdal) to Quebec (Klara du Plessis) to Nova Scotia (Katie Fewster-Yan).

Since we're interested in mentoring editors as well as publishing books, many of the writers who have served on the Anstruther Press editorial board began with little to no editorial experience. As such, I've spent time teaching / learning along with them, discussing poetics, editorial strategies, and the way titles interact within our booklist. In addition to reading submissions that come in by email, board members are encouraged to solicit manuscripts—in this way, Anstruther benefits from having multiple sounding boards to help broaden my personal tastes and ideas about poetry. Over time, we've also become increasingly open to taking recommendations outside of the editorial board proper, acquiring manuscripts through Anstruther alumni like Manahil Bandukwala, Sarah Burgoyne, and Benjamin C. Dugdale. Since the future of any literature hinges on its editors as much as its writers, mentoring mentors remains one of Anstruther's explicit mandates.

Introduction

Inside of a mountain hollowed out

When you hear it, you'll know. Iterative, but without echo. Inside of a mountain hollowed out. There aren't many poets who possess truly original voices, poets who can harness diction and syntax in a way that bends language to their will. Klara du Plessis is this kind of writer. From the very first poem in *Wax Lyrical* (and the first poem in this anthology) it's easy to get swept "forward into the stream" of Klara's mind, a place of such intense clarity that the person she describes showering doesn't wet her hair, but holds wetness in the space between strands. Obsessed with body, ritual, and the line between shame and desire, Klara's early poems cut through the page like an igneous vein bisecting metamorphic rock, often with a force that demands lines be read over and over again.

While each section of *The Anstruther Reader* is arranged chronologically, the choice to open the book with Klara's poetry is deliberate. *Wax Lyrical* is a benchmark, setting the stage for the poet's trademark "linguistic honesty." It was the first Anstruther Press chapbook to be shortlisted for the bpNichol Chapbook Award, and it was also one of the last to be printed without a title on the cover. There, Klara's artwork stands alone on glossy cardstock, bleeding into the poetry itself. I read: "One day I take a little razor and shave it all off," then flip back to see the legs that protrude from a scored black and white background. A shower curtain? Part of the Canadian Shield? The background is unclear, a shifting proposition depending on which poem is referenced.

Up, a spray of green

Enter colour. Matthew Walsh's wall of computer green. Shawn Adrian's ochre prairie. Jenna Lyn Albert's Baroque spray of arterial blood. Just as Anstruther Lake is the source of much of my imaginative world, the poets we publish bring their places to us, giving readers insight into a cross-section of the Canadian imagination. Maybe "place" is the wrong word, since I'm not referring to the term in the parochial way it was conceived during the nation-building era of the 1960s and 1970s, when CanLit lived in the shadow of Margaret Atwood's *Survival* and D.G. Jones's *Butterfly on Rock*. The place that Anstruther poets write through is a liminal space, where metaphor, associative movement, and identity ground the work and the world where it exists.

Jim Johnstone

Take T. Liem's Montreal. When Liem writes about the city, it's refracted through the prism of their interior world. This interiority is distinctly tied to place, as the protagonists in *Tell Everybody I Say Hi* are frequently isolated in rooms and buildings, or at least confined to the limits of their own bodies. Whether T.'s speaker is in a museum-like apartment, looking for their partner on "the other side of the window," or ruminating on the politics of staying home, this is a poetics that's rooted in a world of its own. Different, certainly than Darren Bifford's Montreal hospital ward that resembles purgatory, where "every cause is an effect of a prior cause." It's also separate from the Montreal air that allows Sarah Burgoyne's dancers to "cut thunder" across their bodies, relayed with a physicality that's intentionally absent in *Tell Everybody I Say Hi*.

The liminal and physical also contrast in Amanda Merpaw's *Put the Ghosts Down Between Us*, particularly throughout "The Communist's Daughter." Named after a bar in Toronto, "The Communist's Daughter" cuts between the titular space (where the speaker is on a date) and moments that take place in a future that "exists before it happens." Emotion is held at arms length as the poem unfolds, with the question "Who do you want me to be?" hanging between the protagonists as they share physical intimacies. So much of the poem is anticipated instead of enacted that the speaker seems like a ghost haunting a temporary city. Is this the same Toronto where Kirby slides under a TTC bus in "Kindness?" Both are queer spaces, but they are filtered through lenses that have the power to transform time and place.

When I published *The Next Wave: An Anthology of 21st Century Canadian Poetry* in 2018, I characterized the group of Canadian poets selected to appear in the book as the selfie generation. This cohort had published three books or less at the time, and were adept at bridging the digital divide by synthesizing multiple poetic styles simultaneously. Self-referential and self-assured, their poems moved quickly, as if they employed hyperlinks, "harnessing the echo chamber of the internet into a malleable, impressionistic music." These characteristics still stand in *The Anstruther Reader*, though the poets are different. Read on and you'll find representative samples from sixty Anstruther authors, selected to present the story of the press through the voices that have come to define it.

Introduction

Reading the work that makes up the anthology, I'm left with much the same feeling that I have on the water, navigating Anstruther's corkscrewing wake. Up, a spray of green. Body bobbing into the tree line, again and again. The poems here prize empathy, and display inimitable emotional and metaphorical range with words that are sensed as well as seen. You'll find this in Melissa Schnarr's "dancing light meant to ward away wendigos." The feeling also exists in the necklaces that Fawn Parker's protagonist touches "like harp strings," filling a gift shop with music. The sound diffuse, but acutely felt.

Down, a pitch black eye

In 2018, the Anstruther literary umbrella expanded to include Anstruther Books. For those new to the divide, Anstruther Press is the chapbook press that informs this anthology, and Anstruther Books is an imprint for full-length collections that I select and edit at Palimpsest Press. The imprint gives me the flexibility to work with poets on books that the chapbook press can't accommodate, projects of greater length and scope that are distributed in bookstores across Canada (as opposed to selling exclusively online). Many of the collections in the series come from authors who started with Anstruther Press and were ready to publish full-length books, like Jaclyn Desforges, David Ly, Amanda Merpaw, Tolu Oloruntoba, Fawn Parker, and Klara du Plessis (as well as a forthcoming title by Melissa Schnarr). All are represented here with poems that were originally published in chapbook form.

I didn't envision this future when I was invited to select and edit occasional full-length poetry titles for Palimpsest Press in 2012. Looking down into the pitch black eye of the lake, Anstruther Press hadn't yet been conceived. I took the job at Palimpsest for a specific reason: to publish Marc di Saverio's *Sanatorium Songs*. At the time, Marc's poems were met with antagonism for the qualities that set them apart, including a vehement focus on mental health, his formal mastery, and an Ezra Pound-like kinetic energy so astonishing I still have a hard time deciphering whether Marc is reciting poetry or singing when he performs on stage. He made the jump to Anstruther Press when it formed, first publishing *Death Calls*, and then *Aftersongs*, excerpted in the pages ahead.

The oracle speaks, and is silent. Out of this silence, the Anstruther Books imprint became a reality when Aimee Parent Dunn took the helm as publisher at Palimpsest Press. Aimee encouraged me to assume a larger editorial role (which

Jim Johnstone

has included curating Palimpsest's non-fiction line as well as its poetry line), and to build a dual brand. Historically, Anstruther's dual structure is comparable to past Canadian publishers like Ryerson Press (think Milton Acorn's *The Brain's the Target* and Margaret Avison's *Winter Sun*) or Contact Press (think Louis Dudek's *Twenty-four Poems* and Gwendolyn MacEwen's *The Rising Fire*). In the new century, Anstruther's duality hews more closely to Junction Books, which publishes chapbooks, and once existed as a full-length imprint at Nightwood Editions.

To date, Anstruther Books is most well known for publishing Tolu Oloruntoba's Griffin Poetry Prize and Governor General's Award winning *The Junta of Happenstance*. The origins of that collection are reflected here in three poems reprinted from *Manubrium*. Densely patterned, musical, and embodying Keats's conception of negative capability, this work would be startling if it had been published by an established poet, never mind in a debut chapbook. From the armour on the front cover to the speaker grunting through "the bull run" of their inner ribs in "She Says—," *Manubrium* is the epitome of what Erica and I have aimed to achieve at Anstruther Press, and an exemplar of how we envision our chapbooks translating to full-length collections at Anstruther Books.

An outboard motor

In the fall, the water level drops and Anstruther Lake is transformed, its shallow lakebed revealing geographical features that were hidden when mosquitos and blackflies skimmed its summer surface. Large, algae-covered rocks protrude in shallow waters, and old tree stumps abut the waves. There's an aboutness to the lake at this time, a sense that one can see what was only assumed to lie below previously. Depth becomes a consideration, particularly when boating, and there are times the outboard motor needs to be lifted to avoid rocks near the shore.

Erica and I have focused on poetry exclusively since Anstruther Press began. The only exception to this is writing *about* poetry, which forms our Manifesto Series, edited by Shane Neilson. The series was inspired by a chapbook of Shane's own, *The Manifesto of Fervourism*, which exhorts poets to write with fervour across four points:

Introduction

1) Choose the emotional life.

2) Emotion must be dynamic.

3) Be the emotion that others wish they felt.

4) Seek to affect others with fervourism.

These are components of the engine that makes poetry run. Look into the lake and emotion is the wake that follows the swimmers, the leg kicks that carry them forward. Poetry is special in part because of its depth of feeling, the ability of the form to amplify love, desire, awe, and anger in compressed stanzas. Poetry can "command a regiment of horse and lance to raze a village." Or, without Shane's metaphor from *The Manifesto of Fervourism*, poetry can collapse time and space to allow readers to feel the army of words at a writer's disposal.

Shane's argument for emotion in poetry urged Erica and I to take on the Manifesto Series under his guidance. Though "manifesto" is a loaded term in the 21st century, our explicit aim is to look for arguments that make poetry more accessible, more accommodating of difference. To date, we're published manifestos that argue that "the Beauty of nature is Truth" (M. Travis Lane), that poetry exists as spectacle (Yusra Usmani), and that poetry is akin to both living to work and working to live (Robert Colman). We've also published pieces like John Nyman's *Slogan, Substance, Dream*, which is as much a poem itself as it is a discussion of the author's investment in "an open poetry." Whether I agree with the opinions expressed in these pieces or not, each one serves as a spark plug quickening the pulse of poetic discourse.

The black dock

I'm often asked about the future of Anstruther Press. Will we expand? Will we modify our production standards and begin to print perfect bound books? Will we seek out a distributor to pitch our titles to bookstores? The truth is: I'd like to get smaller. I've always thought of micropress as a punk rock form of bookmaking, and I still feel close to the teenager who used to cobble together inky zines in the basement of my parents' home. To wit: after ten years, Anstruther

Jim Johnstone

Press still publishes chapbooks without contracts, relying on handshakes to certify commitment.

The flexibility of micropress is paramount to the Anstruther Press aesthetic. I couldn't have started the press without the ability to learn through trial and error, a fluid production schedule, or the freedom to add new initiatives as our journey has progressed. Currently, we publish around twenty chapbooks a year, including the titles in our Manifesto Series. Going forward, Erica and I plan to keep moving in an impressionistic, instinctual manner, taking on what we can publish when we can publish it. I expect that will mean publishing less in the long term, but continuing to publish with intention.

This intention carries us forward to the edge of the black dock. From the water there's a stand of trees, a forest. You can see the cabin where I'm writing this, the overhanging rocks that lead deeper into the woods, then the swamp beyond. I've rarely ventured farther—the mosquitos get too thick, and it's difficult terrain. Still, we'll continue to travel this kind of terrain with our authors, since our existence is predicated on the community of writers and editors who have trusted us with their work, and who have proved they care about poetry, even on the smallest scale. Anstruther Press continues, and the future is now. Even so, I don't like to predict. Balance is never achieved for long.

Anstruther Lake
2024

Black Ash

First Chapbooks

Klara du Plessis

The pragmatism of a girl entering a room, drying her hands the eroticism of a girl drying her hair, head bent

Contrary to common belief, hair cannot get wet.
I wash with my head bent forward beneath the faucet
sweeping forward into the stream, abstracting the nape to a line.
The lines of my hair all singular.
Collectively immersed in water, there is a wetness,
but still each hair, taken separate, is solid.
Solids dissolve, do not let water pass through them.
It is the division between strands then, which is wet,
and creates the illusion of drench.
Same with a shirt. It is the spaces between the threads I clean.

Klara du Plessis

Wax lyrical

One day I take a little razor and shave it all off.
Looking obscenely young, I admire myself,
head bent or staring forward in a mirror.
Cool and young and sexy,
I'm available, stripped to possibility.
Discover me or I need to discover myself.
For in the shower every drop of water is felt.
I am exposed and experience it as an intrusion.
Hair is an extra layer of skin, a means not to feel.
Being now so naked I sense my modesty even with clothes on.
Edge a blade across my most intimate skin,
a clean, marble look, with a slight rose glow.
By evening, there is a blue tinge,
little heads below the skin,
a female five o'clock shadow.
Shaving then isn't an option.
It speeds growth and thickens the bush.
It leaves a latent feel of uncleanliness.

I try waxing a stylish square of hair.
Return to a woman where I don't mind unfolding my legs.
She touches without fearing the smell of me.
Obviously one showers comprehensively
before such an intimate appointment.
She cleans me up and pats me dry like a baby.
But after, the sides are red,
the pores stand out,
bruised,
little specks of blood where tough hairs were extracted,
discolorations in the soft folds between thigh and pelvis,
a bikini wax gone wrong, the sensitivity
of my pubis renders it unsightly.
After a number of days the region temporarily
settles into cinematic perfection.
Before the hair grows out, still too short to redo.

Klara du Plessis

There's an acid lotion that eats away the hair.
You smear it on like cream,
wait,
scrape it off with a pink plastic tool,
scared to burn your fingers
while lathering it directly on intimacy.
It stinks of putrefaction and dissolution of tissue.
Why complain, professionals say,
laser hair removal is permanent.
Permanence sounds traditional. I flee.

Initially when I decided to tidy up pubic hair,
I was told, there are styles, you need to choose an identity.
Do you want nothing,
a strip of hair,
a pattern?
If you leave some, will it be trimmed or naturally curled?
People like to say, au naturel, as if it's funny
or an aesthetic choice to be yourself.
Hair has a life of its own. It splits,
devilish,
two hairs per root.
It bursts through the surface, pubescence vying with maturity.
Or it won't grow at all, sticking beneath the skin,
a type of pelvic acne. I read somewhere,
who cares, just pop them as you'd do on your face
I'm shocked, can't believe what I see.

It's all about surface.
To do with connecting the inner and outer planes
of body, while also destructing
the flatness of skin.
When hair is removed, uniformity is installed.
Feeling the leg, so smooth, but empty.
One-sided touch, a hand running along skin,
but body not reaching back.

Klara du Plessis

Surface can mean that which is obvious,
or that which is not obvious at all.

Like the area of my visible body, a first superficial layer.
Like what still needs to surface, what is hidden deeper.
It's in submission then, with a gesture of penitence,
that one day I start removing my body hair one by one,
plucking each out with a pair of tweezers.
The guilt of imperfection weighs me down.
I sense that my body is in the wrong.
It should be crystal clear.

Klara du Plessis

Dream in radical disclosure

It is during sleep that I experience intense release.
Before, the pressure on my bladder is very strong
I can barely keep it in.
Like when I'm having sex without peeing in advance
and is it pleasure or pressure.
I know I should get up to look
desperately for the washroom.
Looking, looking, I have lost something.
Walking about feeling vastly uncomfortable.
Why are those girls looking at me?
What have I ever done to them? Nothing.
Or maybe I can't remember?
I don't even know who they are.
I don't even know who I am.
But I find hair everywhere.
In food.
In new books.
In the drains of my room.
A place so familiar, its public lavatory seems clean.
If I had someone to phone here, I'd phone her up.
Feel me up.
Wake me up.
Am I awake?
I'm awake, I say.
Sure I'm awake, I say.
Absolutely sure I'm awake, I say.
That's good, great in fact, that's great news, I say.
Because I see a urinal upfront.
Don't worry, women can use the men's lavatory
sometimes. Unisex toilets
always have the seats forgotten vertical, or wet.
This is stressful.
Am I sure I'm awake?
I don't know, do something, check, I say.
Like what, I say.

Klara du Plessis

I don't know, like pee a little, see if I'm on a seat, I say.
Really, can I do that?
Live a little, I say.
Live like liver.
The most alive I've been.
Like awake.
Do it.
I can do it.
Then the release.
The most intense sense of release.
The pressure is less, I'm so grateful for finding this place.
Things feel so good now.
It's pathetic that things don't always feel this good,
I should really make an effort to relax more often.
It's not right, how under pressure I always am.
I should really concentrate more on the little pleasures.
Like then I'd know when something feels right.
Something isn't right.
I'm not awake, I say.
How do you mean I'm not awake?
You even said I'm awake, I say.
Well I'm not awake, I say.
But now I'm awake, I say.
Now you tell me.
Wet.
Shit, the sheets too.
I wake up so often at night these days.
What's this about?
I used to sleep all the way through.
All these bathroom breaks.
Or whatever this is.
Ripping off the bedding.
Getting right back into bed.
Getting right back into myself.

Bardia Sinaee

Wireless Fidelity

He said go get your kicks somewhere else.
He said why not try *this* on for size.
A warm gust jostles the blinds and light seeps into the room.
In all this is no measure of humility,

for it was meant to turn out this way, with a bucket of ice
and some quack from the island,
his nebula of acne scars lending the dalliance
a brutish air, with an inkling, too,

of something remotely dangerous.
The ochre sky is dark around the edges, like a big sliced plum
behind the landing planes
that drown out the Chevy's phlegmy rumble

as it nears. Starved anticipation
brought them here, where the roads
all lead to water, and all the cellphone towers
go offline during a storm.

Bardia Sinaee

Sonnet

You're getting back into the swing of things:
Seasons, days of the week,
Geraniums restored to the sill
To wring their colours
In the sun-swabbed afterthought of a storm.

Life had become a secret room
And whether I found you laughing or lashing out
It was to reconcile with living
Your want of a motive.

Meanwhile the wind spread ashes like snow upon the landscape,
Obscuring the fugitive trails
So that whoever had been planning cautiously to set forth
Might think themselves the first
And be emboldened.

Bardia Sinaee

The Weather

What else is there to say about
the weather, which has seemed
a veiled, remote experiment
all winter? Relayed by the jet stream,
air that cut its teeth along the Tombstone Range

is ransacking the belfry
of the Church of the Holy
Protection. Heat loss draws
the pigeons shuddering on its roof
as if they might abscond with the cross.

Ice imbues the puddles
with a cling-wrap sheen, inscribes
elaborate fern motifs on window panes
and fractures into tangrams underfoot.
The priest scratches the salt stain on his shoe,

extends his hand and says
I'm sorry for your loss. Because
what else is there to say? The mourners
slip and catch each other on the concrete steps
and cross themselves before they cross the street.

Allison LaSorda

Coven

Till I was sixteen, I thought Sylvia Plath
put her head in a lit oven.

I've never wanted anything
enough to let my face melt off.

In the evening, I pick my stigmata
scab, and show myself out.

At most, I slap my face
three times and come like Beetlejuice.

It's the *why not* that stings.

Picture blisters, raw waffle-iron cheeks
and how stubborn I'd rather be.

My beard of bees mourns
razor burn in a sallow sink.

I've not wanted plenty, a dead dad,
arts asking too much from their faker.

Allison LaSorda

Playdate

You've got me where you want me
but what wants are left are paltry;
I've bailed, searching out the lick
in the split crow footprint of your spit,
left to dry white astride my thighs.
Let me rinse this off and watch
what scenes crop up in the fray
of each time you couldn't come out.
Playing with you is like teaching
a humpback whale how not to breach.

Allison LaSorda

Fish & Bird

The smallest cut has the fewest needs,
least of all attention. The largest cut's
requirements surpass our abilities.
It is impossible to find unless stumbled
upon, and then proves challenging to categorize.
Recognizable as flesh, is not slash or butterfly,
lance or scrape; neither prepared event nor accident.
It exists between, a split not quite in twain.
The largest cut possesses unreachable depths
and blind, frightening fish. It's unlimited closets,
hidden attics, shake with captured wind
from flapping birds' wings. To call it a sinkhole
wouldn't be totally wrong. The smallest cut
is your childhood and every memory a splinter.
The largest cut is your unused potential, a void
beckoning with ancestral moans like everything
you couldn't say, and everything you did.

T. Liem

At the museum without you

I wanted to ask
if you thought
the painting of a room
wanted to be a room.

The bed made,
curtains tied in a knot,
a towel hanging
on an open door

because you left
as if you would return.
At the museum I'm left looking
for you in an empty room.

I walked toward the painting
like a diver on the platform,
slow steps in a straight line,
all my attention breathing in.

You didn't appear in the light,
or the line of its shadow.
You were not on the other side
of the window. You were

not even in the texture of the paint.
If you don't come back soon,
I want to be a high diver
the moment after her feet disappear

& find you in the smallest air,
a bubble floating to the surface.

T. Liem

Everything I do is political, especially when we stay home

I want to leave the house in the clothes I sleep in
& not need to go home again.

But I am not well enough to leave
not well enough to sleep

& so when I stay home
everything I do is political

because I've been reading
about the ethics of space & because

sometimes I lie on the floor
until you text me asking me why I'm not out

& because sometimes we have sex
with most of our clothes on.

Sometimes we lie
on the floor

& text everybody
who is out asking:

> *why aren't you home
> being political?*

We stay in
& keep our bodies ethical

so to speak. We know if we go out,
we will dress for the street.

T. Liem

Work

We make our hands work
in terribly ordinary ways.

Out
in the park we adjust our hemlines because
there is no nice way to sit
in a summer dress.

We lean back on our palms
until they are etched with grass.

I point to clouds
tracing shapes in the sky
& you pick enough dandelions
to make yourself bracelets.

If we laugh
we cover our mouths with our hands.

Shazia Hafiz Ramji

Sense

We have come to the summit of our distance.
Blue-flecked, temperature of scalp on the third floor.
Footfalls fall on by the cemetery gate.
A hush in the running from what-we-can't-know—
From what we can't know there exudes.
A there in the summit of our presence.
The grooves of deixis, only until—
Who will carry us?
We are fluid and must be contained.
To be seen we must be held.
Succulent on the nape, soft and ready.
We once thought we could feel across each other.
We were once called mad.
But we have spoken and in words have made it come:
    "Effluvia"
    "Ghost in the machine"
    "Automata"
    "Influencing-machine"
We sit here waiting for the threshold, waiting for sense.
Blue-flecked, temperature of scalp on the third floor.

Shazia Hafiz Ramji

An Ambulance Speaks to Coyotes

I think about myself a lot—what will you think of me? I'm not someone who can call on a postmodern "I" brought to you by their psychoanalyst via Skype in Los Angeles. I will always be working class; I can't drop a move like that in the p.m. You need to know I think about myself a lot—I think of you. At two a.m. when the ambulance goes by and all the coyotes in the ravine go nuts, I am still thinking of you. I think of you a lot. What will you think of me if I tell you that all I want to do is talk to you. Isn't this what it's all about? Please look at me—I have punched in a long em dash every time I talk about myself and then talk about you. It has come to this—yes, we are connected by an em dash. I want to talk to you. Listen, those coyotes are howling. It's not two in the morning, but an ambulance has gone by and they think it's one of them. Listen to this noise I'm making. There is nothing conceptual about it, unless of course, you are either a coyote or the ambulance, or both, otherwise you would not be wondering what I am talking about.

Shazia Hafiz Ramji

Fundamentally Caring

after Philip Seymour Hoffman

He tells me "you are fundamentally, caring."
I had just finished talking about Phil

in *Magnolia*, the Sufi at the tea shop said
he is fundamentally happening, like

liking. One to another—likening
the fish in the pond to movements

of the self against the viscosity of
it. Being me, I sit on the bench,

stroke my thumb against the upper
part of my other self, fins

moving at the same pace as I
pay my debt to the dead by desiring
                    to feel the same.

Emily Skov-Nielsen

Volta

Meet me at the volta, the high-voltage tulips' canary-
coloured trance supervened by a spell, a turning

away of attention, intention—what is hypnosis?
I mean rose hip gnosis, red and pluck-worthy

they were on that bitumen black night at Bear Cove
where you bit into the fruit's hip, into its hairs,

while I rambled on about King Tut's meteorite knife
and X-Ray fluorescence, the two of us harebrained

in a warm blizzard of juvenescence, the moon
a puzzle of orbital bones, or was it a wolf spider's

egg sac? Round silken globe lighting the starflowers
at our feet, the terraqueous space of water and land,

chaos and cosmos—did someone say subaqueous,
subconscious? The red of your sweater was all over

me and tut-tut went the tip-of-the-tongue phenomenon,
and all I could think of was a pic of the tip of a tulip

stamen in our grade ten bio textbook, and how you
pinched the skin below my breast alerting my attention

to the almost-rhyme, *stamen, semen*, and the wet shock
of spit that followed from your laugh, landing on my bare

shoulder, spaghetti-strapped, open for business, the first
in a series of disillusions, I mean dissolutions—was I

Emily Skov-Nielsen

the solvent or you? Repeat after me: *solvō*, Latin for loosen,
untie, undo—when the sweat and the red was all over,

the tit-for-tat, or something like that, the word re-
turned to me at last like an old friend I no longer knew.

Emily Skov-Nielsen

Menstromania

Loose and bloody in the bathwater, a crossbred
sea star/sponge/jellyfish of mucosal tissue,

a strand of uterus, a small stringed instrument,
a nest, a tuft of down feather fallen from a bird

in the hand of my body (a hedge sparrow)—
or maybe it's a knot of spider silk. It is time

spelled out—f-o-u-r weeks to be exact; a shredded page
from a calendar eaten by the moon whose teeth

shine as it bites through my lower abdomen, a pain
lit from the inside like a paper lantern—yes,

this is what my body has become overnight,
a ranting lunatic of clarity and impulse, dysphoria

and cravings—a bloated hull, red sky at morning,
an eyelid turned inside out, a dauntless sea-craft

crossing waters in an equatorial counter current
spurred by monsoon winds—wind spiking

the ocean's surface like a dragon fruit; my body
is the red rind of a tart, hidden pomegranate,

the air is appetite, tonguing the pulpy seeds
(*of what?*) inside me, inciting a slow evisceration,

catabolization, breakdown in the bloodstream,
the hemodynamics of the world, its nonstop

pulse searching for the aortic semi-lunar valve
in the arterial tree, a big-tooth aspen perhaps,

Emily Skov-Nielsen

yes, that's the one. Don't call me hysteric, call me
wisteric, bearing racemes of blue-lilac papilionaceous

flowers and wrist-thick trunks, collapsing latticework.
I'm a head case with an acute associative disorder

tending a garden of hypochondriasis with offshoots
of violet amnesias, long convoluted tendrils climbing

a trellis of intersecting stakes—I'm a recovering psycho-
somatic somnambulating between the body and the mind,

rebuilding the distance with words until relapsing
into this poem, this unmoored monastery of endometrial

cells adrift, this intertidal rag-bag tatter of home, no longer
a home but a memory—far and near, loose and bloody.

R.P. LaRose

Under the Snow

∞

Seeds glow on the crystals plain
and to the big eyes, so do I.

In my subnivean
I dream of the blood above
in the breath of all forms of mean.

To run each day and never travel far
I must be as silent as the big eyes' seamless flight—
a patch that flits but never flickers
through paths in flakestars.

Above the crust sky stars screech
as they divulge the presence
on a branch earing me

as my pulse drums up to a sink of sound.

A catching face.

Memory please stay near

as long as I remember they are there—
as long as I never move—
I'll be here

R.P. LaRose

∞

What's outside the bedroom window
looks inside.

Things howl out there
and in bed underneath light movements
a blanket roils.

We move uniformly entangled from window
to window in the moon prairie mountains and foothills,

a milk landscape where
we shutter doors and screens
that utter against us,

our house a body of woods
pulled like teeth from children
and their perfectly possible futures
and of steel and a snake also pulled
from underneath the house, not far away

R.P. LaRose

A Dream in the Bush While Living on Fish

∞

When I cut the steak I didn't see, coiled in the flesh, three steel curves with barbs tethered by line to sky. I forked them plate to mouth in a seared cube. The invisible length tautened. Steel escaped meat and two points slid through my upper gums. One sunk between canine and incisor. The other shattered molar and root. A third sliced my tongue, bottom jaw, and septum. Something from the blue world jerked me from my chair, knocking over the table and scattering guests like carp. My body shattered the glass ceiling, hook dislocating jaw and shards falling to the floor like thin-bladed knives. Steel ejected more teeth in spurts of blood. Air thinned and blue loomed beyond troposphere

R.P. LaRose

Some Words Held in a Love Poem

∞

Some mornings we were too heavy
so we lifted us together.

Shadows leaned in across
industrial oceans and closing borders
like ones you crossed to
save us and I cross
to be home with you
us—two people in a wooded blizzard holding hands.

Womxn and men exist but
only in sentences.

    We could be words in those sentences.

Held to each other
semantics and grammar

our sentences could read:
    "I love me
    therefore
    I love you"

they read

"chameleon
can only be
one set of images at a time"

but change comforts me

David Ly

Stubble Burn

1.

You wait for him over coffee
because it is innocent so long
as you keep adding sugar.
Sorry I'm late. The last
time he apologized, you turned
yourself into an ex. Keep it innocent.
Keep it innocent. Don't stop
adding sugar. Add sugar.
Add sugar. Add sugar.

2.

Your mind wanders to how it felt
to spend time in a room that has
never really left you. You
recall giving him too many sweat-laced
secrets. Before you could lick them all
back from his lips, you notice the
glass of water hasn't fallen
off the nightstand and onto the mattress
so maybe it's all going to be worth it.

3.

So you take him in, his tongue
kind between your thighs.
You're so my type is lovely
in the moment because that's
just how romance works. But
when he cums inside, you want
to leave your body. Water spills
onto the mattress. He drips out
of you. Drips. Drips. Drips.

David Ly

4.

Doggy-style, doggy-breath. He
compliments your *amazing ass*
in the heat. He helps you
finish with a bite here, here, there.
I'm your rice queen slips through
his teeth and you swallow salty
love. If cum splatters can be
read like tea leaves yours are
shaped like black beetles.

5.

Your skin begins to crawl. His
words hit you when he meant
for them to kiss. He kisses
your sweaty brow and moves
down your neck. His stubble
burns in a way you can't stand.
A lump forms in your throat and
to stay calm you focus on un-syncing
your breathing from his.

6.

You feel bigger than the skin that
holds you, which he worships. *Can
we still have coffee tomorrow?* You
promise yourself that's all you
will have with him from now
on. So long as you keep conversation
innocent, say only what you want,
not what you think he would like. Speak
less sweetly. Less sweet. Less sweet.

David Ly

I Just Wanted a Blue Hawaiian

      Lady Gaga gives a million reasons
to dance closer to the emptiness
shattered open by a Long Island from slippery fingers,
but I stay at the bar half-shouting
              to the lip-syncing bartender
to get his attention. I want
      a Blue Hawaiian instead.
A hand cut from marble
reaches past me to pay for my drink. I turn, putting
tongue to teeth, but he winks
      before a word slips from my sweat-laced lips.
His monster's jawline and cerulean-eyed kindness
makes me wonder if he did it because
      he wants to know me
or knows there are millions of me.

David Ly

White+++

Asian
selected
from
drop
down
menu

only
drops
pants
for
tops
seeking
gaysians

Lily Wang

In Hope

When love comes I forget
my rules, they are just theory.
In practice my temperature
is always apocalyptic, words
cannot break through me.
I am deaf in this shine.
Stumbling gracelessly toward
the pinnacle of desire
as if this was not a journey
I'd made before. And of course
I'd give it all up. I'd grab
the hot knife if I were cold
enough. I'm crowded
with language, stomping
my boots on your mat.
There's no shame in being
welcomed.

Lily Wang

Mood Ring

I am a violet mist under the bed
sheets / when the covers lift
green moss / sun trap / down
rising / my pillow stuffed
with spirits / I sit up /
let the light bleed through me /
the colours in my ring shift /
just like that / bleed through me

Lily Wang

To Recap:

What happened is the roof was leaking
so we went and got some buckets
but it was Icarus falling from the sun
and the water was from his father's eyes,
and we were tired from all this coming
and going so each of us took some wax
and made little wax-hats, and some of us
put a feather on the brim, and some
of us changed our minds, and some of us
got bored, so we breathed onto our hands
and rubbed our palms against the wall
until all the etchings were gone,
but we really should have been wearing shoes
if we were going to be up to our knees in salt.

Fawn Parker

Golden Rays of Chemo

A large left lump
Skewing the skin like
A sickle like a stump like a
A weak spot in a balloon

The broken latex over shellac
The oil in the ocean
The come
        And go

2017
was the summer
of my mother's breasts!

Golden rays of chemo

Washing

Chamomile and lemon juice

The dog walker left forbidden fruit
On the kitchen island

Let her have some fun,
she said,
A bird in the hand
Is a flat straight line

Fawn Parker

Strawberry Thief

1.

We disagreed,
My mother and I,
though we were both wrong.

I saw it as a precious red gem,
she a black spider.

It was changing,
shrinking,
always,
anyway.

Unless it wasn't. Then we were in trouble.

We used the phrase "100% cancer-free,"
all of us.

The surgeon,
myself,
my mother.

This was our vision.

My mother laughed and applied her makeup.

She talked freely about death.

Fawn Parker

2.

In the mirror in the stranger's bathroom,
I looked like my mother.

There was genetic testing available to determine if I had
"the gene."

If so, this was the situation:
50/50.

I pulled at the fabric over my navel,
baring my breasts to myself.

Snake eyes.

Fawn Parker

3.

You know what Claire Danes said?
said Emilie,
That actor? she said.

"Acting is the greatest answer to my loneliness."

If I had the gene they would take my uterus.
But if I conceived quickly before my operation?

The gene,
the gene.

Imagine if I were to pass it on.

At least I wouldn't be lonely.

At least there would be
someone at my breast.

Fawn Parker

In the Gift Shop

In the gift shop
I touch necklaces like harp strings.

The girl you slept with,
Her name is on everything.

A plastic surfboard
A hibiscus mug
A small grain of rice inside of a dolphin.

I buy a keychain
Her name on a rubber palm tree

For my sister, I say to the clerk
Who does not ask

Sister,
Did he choke you too

I know you were too drunk
To get wet

By the water
You are teaching me
How to skip rocks

I throw the keychain and it sinks

Oubah Osman

Horner Hybridity

for all Somali women

You stem from me in all forms,
stream from me in all places.
You and I,

long stretched
Us over continents.

Us, together, landscape bodies and sinkhole eyes,
Us, together, open cityscapes, open wounds.
We are the gun and also the martyr.

Sometimes, we expand, like Shebelle.
Sometimes, we fall simple and sudden, like Assal,

but there are ways to be two and also to be one,
ways to know you, and then to know you again.

Oubah Osman

Drop

after Cornelius Eady's Brutal Imagination

When I die it's like I'm sitting in the backseat of your car.
The air rolls over me
and the warm vagueness of I simmers;
all of me a gesture towards dying.

When I die, I die inside of the backseat of your car.
I count backwards into the lonely road.
My heart tunnels out and you look on from a blinking
light that points east.

When I die my eyes are sealed, lash
to lash. I braid myself against time.

In the car I am inside of a humming body.
Red lights coat me. In passing they turn white hot.
In the backseat there are murmurs, a rumbling
and then a quick drop.

When I think about dying, I think about God
clapping His hands just once, and all of us falling,

one by one, into a memory.
I trace myself along this memory,
watch my heart aim itself outward,
take on shapes, until I drop again.

Oubah Osman

Hereditary Blue

The night my mother died she was tending to the garden in the gloom of our broken porch light. I called to her and asked why she was knee-deep in the dirt. She called back, "Women are red until men turn them blue."

I was lazy from the meal she had made so I didn't get up to ask what she meant, and I thought nothing of the small rushing noise from the hose. It was my sister who came downstairs to ask where our mother had gone. Before I could answer, she was already opening the door to check the garden. All at once, my mother floated into the living room on a tide of sinking blues and yellows, her wrists grinning like twin Cheshire cats. I watched as the colours made their way through our halls and into our basement. I didn't know what to say.

It took us a week to drain the house. We cried with for the memory of her body emptying, and the garden that would go unloved.

No matter how hard we tried, we could never completely erase that night. Each room held memories of the flood. Between the tiles there were hints of periwinkle and dimples of red. Cabinets lined themselves in rainbow. We lit uunsi to drive away the madness.

Months later, when I asked my great-grandmother in a dream why my mother used her gardening scissors that way, she said, "My daughter held those hues inside of her until one day she couldn't hold onto them any longer. Her body was so heavy with them." She paused to survey me with her indigo eyes. "And could you imagine carrying all of that around, Yo-Yo? Wouldn't you want to be just a little lighter?"

The next morning I stand in the shower for so long that I think I see pools of purple curve around each of my toes. When I shake away the colours, they expand to blue. I shut my eyes and see blue. I water the plants and see them bloom blue. Something about this presence picks me up and throws me against a wall. I wake up with that blue song in my head, telling me there is nothing else but this insistent colour. Nothing else but this.

Manahil Bandukwala

Rosewater

Fixtures of a volatile city

on the coast of a country
rising and falling
with the tide. Three steps

backward for every five
taken forward.
Progress at a standstill.

The *fresh* in *fresh*
spring of water
out of place in the box

of a bedroom where stale air
settles into furniture.
Even dust doesn't rise.

Only the brief cadence
of raised voices, drunks
roaming downtown

on Tuesday night.
Gunshots worm
their way into every place

eventually. Blues
and reds hide
in wallets, in socks,

in letters from lovers
that find their way back
from the recycling bin.

Manahil Bandukwala

To Be Important

Witness
first kiss
First
ocean shore

Human bones
breaking
into wolf

Calendar
of millennia

Cauldrons tucked
in grottos
moonbeams
squeezing
through cracks

We swim
in waves

Clandestine

Never where
lovers meet

Manahil Bandukwala

I can't shelve my race to study for a midterm

Spots pepper a quail's egg the way a snail
crawls to incrementally bigger shells
smallest ones inhabited briefly   but only
a few go beyond size of big toe. A preserved

flower only stays pristine when no light touch
needs to feel the orange or the folds of a rose

like breeze that breaks thorns off one day
at a time. Yell about beautiful forevers
without touching the white weighted paper
hiding   always hiding. Put ugly thoughts

where we keep all the ugly things. Keep walls
for Instagram   everything succulent

geometric   the next trending hashtag. Once
untouchable   now exotic. Always remember
animals are not for humans and your language
is not for you. Your tongue can't bear the music.

Calmness eludes some people for eternity
others assume their privilege   in bliss.

Jaclyn Desforges

Lacuna

At midnight, I flick the porchlight
and catch a possum in the flood,
three babies clinging to her back,
moon-eyed. At birth, they're small
as honeybees. Did you know that?
Thirteen to a teaspoon begins
their odyssey swimming
the mainland of belly to pouch.
But this isn't about a possum,
or about seeing that possum spooked
in my apple tree, or about peering
over the edge at death, glass
fragments of sad old story pricking
the raw-edged soles of my feet.
It's not about my daughter staring
up from my breast, gulping, or
the thousand ways I've seen her die
in the three years she's been alive.
It's the rest of it – the biannual
scrubbing of the outdoor windows,
that porch at dusk with dry Riesling
in a chilled glass, listening to cicadas
with a hand on my knee, watching her
string up paper flowers and feeling
the graze of light sunburn.

Jaclyn Desforges

In Which an Incel Steps on a Snail

The world flows inside my shell
and out again. You think I'm afraid
but I like the dark.
I have no ears.

You like to imagine me retracted,
every impulse curtailed, divine justice,
something punished.

But nothing stalks me. Only you, your dirty sneakers.
You want to curl up too. You resent the slippery hollow
of my making.

Love, I'm sorry you don't carry
your home on your back.

There are no pink tongues to taste you,
no bodies to coil. No slick membranes to dart
but your own.

Would you like to crush me?
You can't.

The only suffering in this forest is yours.
I appear and recede with your moon.

I like the way you feel, hovering over me,
and the sun and the soil like you too, and the wind,
it likes the way your face is set. Open and closed at once,
an appeal, a spectre.

You think you were made for nothing, exempt from this wildness,
a wilted mistake of your cruel imagined Nature.

Jaclyn Desforges

But don't despair. One of my sisters will save you --
slip inside the coiled mouth of your ear,
nibble a hollow, let the light in.

Jaclyn Desforges

Home Address

I know you, he says, and he's wrong.

Somewhere inside her there is a forest
and in the forest there is a meadow
and in the meadow there is a cottage

and in the cottage she's peeling potatoes
and boiling water for soup.

Confident of her whereabouts in a way
only a man can be confident,

he's two towns over at the abandoned church
pounding on the door.

Jason Purcell

The Spore Collector

*There is no word for the 'floating' gender
in which we would all like to rest.*
—Anne Carson

Not in the jam that sticks the lid.
Never under the thumb, the butter, kneading.

Not here on the shoulder do I know you, gender,
even though you took a bit away from me,

some threads on a nail on the fence
that divides this from that, genital-height

and rigid. Not here do you make longing
out of absence. It sleeves on.

A voice careens through the house. I catalogue
spores and motes, things as small as I am,

while the dog goes outside to hump
something. Back then all of the grandmothers

wore suits in secret
and boys like me grew up somewhere else.

Jason Purcell

Bird House

The floor that is leaving.
The floor that is at our sides.
The floor that creaks until we step on it.

The window in the floor
you pull birds from,
birds that fly inside themselves
and pop in the black hole of this house.

You watch them fly smaller and smaller,
vanish into the air, to some other dimension,
to the front garden behind you,
where you left your shoes,
your bare feet feathered.

Jason Purcell

Men in the Gut

Scrape the inside of sleep the belly wall
tasting like yoghurt cooked broccoli
its emptiness leaving something
on the tongue. Escaping the body
that wants to quit from the inside.
It unlaces you all the tethers sliced
away. When I dream of this body ending
of opening the germ of the pain
I am on the side of the road. My hands
hold out my stomach my second brain
to the men who already want me to die.
This failing organ with a ruby wound
kissing the place it is so easy to be
stabbed or shot. A punch to the gut
I anticipate violence here one cell layer
deep shallow spreading roots
a memory system in my body.
On the side of the road a drive-by for men
homophobic in trucks swallowing spit.
When I was a teenager I let them
disembody me internalizing everything
through the mouth and now my stomach
wants it out. I am interested in self-
diagnosis. When I dream it is of trees
budding from my stomach
that will shade all the wounded men
who masculinity failed
who will lay their Oilers caps on my wrists
say *I'm sorry* and our fingers
will touch without their being afraid.

Tolu Oloruntoba

If Tildes Approximate Wings for the Barrel I'm In

If sweat from my rambling
makes a moat after
the invitation of windowpane sparrows
to jump,
I will be saved.

If a tilde and twin approximate wings ~O~ for the barrel I'm in,
if the tattoo of feet becomes serpent black on a songbook lattice,
if the bunched fingers in a barbed fence are pruned into epileptic
runes in a vèvè of blood, I will be saved.

I will be saved I
will be saved say
the word I will be saved.

The maneuvers of Leopold's amputees, querying a pregnant sky
are practice, too;
the coaxing of sap quick enough,
palms cupping
a Belgian bowl is prayer, too;

and fasciculations of wrist muscles, timing the echolalia of ask
are clapping, too. And if in the grocery store of bewilderment,
I can stock my basket with oil, if I am an adobe hut, matchstick-red,
and the dissident strikes the walls within,

bending terra-cotta
knees
before the light,

if the gauntlet of space junk
round the planet reflects, repeats
my immolation
to me in an offset twinkle of smelt,
ashes, to dust, to glass eye,
Zeiss ball, if I can still see then, even dim, I will be saved.

Tolu Oloruntoba

In Which I, Again, am Fighting My Way Out of Things

Submerged into words on the bus, I sink,
lances of spring light fenestrating
the darkroom of my eye. All
the buses of this route
are fused into multiverse,
mitochondrial microcosm
on the miniature Pennsylvania Rail.
One of these things is not like
the others: it hyperventilates
for a dive into macadam,
sending sonar for the blowhole
of this town. I can tell you now—
my oath was always hypocritical—
I only wanted exit keys for that citadel,
a Heracles butterknifing my way out
of the trash disposal belly
of filial duty, rotor teeth tapering
into ribbons of lead. On ground,
I let the light of a cheeto sun raise
my serotonin, seek lift from the thumb,
the teat of helium tanks,
concentrators of lower density,
and await my summons,
the splintered instructions I must write.

Tolu Oloruntoba

She Says—

don't forget to breathe.
I grunt through
the bull run of my inner ribs,
my lungs a muslin sheath
of drum,
stagger off the panic bus,
pulled over, my night a drunk tank.

Here before my pill—
the fleet of plungers in my brain
ready to sail. Do we
need a prayer, or the like,
for this launch?

I've read the warnings:
this sertraline can reach
and slash your wrists.
But my dark foil is only
a suicide note
if it succeeds. Stop
when you find yourself
baying at the moon.

The elixir demands
scrapings from a sundial's millennial face,
from the skidmarks of its hours.

Autonomy texts show my skull sliced
open after, for ventilation.
The brain has no nerves of its own
so I feel none
of the disrobed ants, their clothes
crackling with light. They wear
only boots of dry ice and pneumatic drills.

Tolu Oloruntoba

Their mother is the wedding of depth
gauges, diviner, a wrecking ball of lie-detector eyes
and jawbones.
I want her to reveal
the secret of blood,
how saplings questionmark
the morning above ground.

She says—

Terese Mason Pierre

Treatment

Rain means your call,
a long sigh into the receiver.

You say the rain makes you
think of the city,

how we are all each other
and nothing;

you are purposeful
in your elegy of islands.

I refuse to ask
if you need anything;

I know you will insist
I am the answer,

and my legs will locate the will
to kneel before your threshold,

soaking my jeans on
your wet doormat.

In May, I go to Grenada
and surrender myself to the sun.

You call to collect
me. I say I am

a different kind of water, a wet
that wonders how we are nothing.

You joke that you're upset
we're not seeing the same sky.

Terese Mason Pierre

I rub dry sand
on my skin—

it must be a season
that never goes away.

Terese Mason Pierre

Lines

You know where you're going,
but this city is unfamiliar to me.

Every story you tell has its own
highways and cul-de-sacs,

leading to laughs you cut short,
a brief peer over the hedge

to the green on the other side,
or a welcome overstayed

on purpose. It is irrational
to envy the time before I existed.

In the attic of your childhood home,
I see you in the orange glow

of a lack of someone to please.
I put my hand over yours

as you hold a photo. I do not
recognize any of the thousand words.

Alison Braid-Fernandez

On Some Good Days

Mornings raise up on stilts
and stalk away. There's a tractor,
a dog in dandelions. A stranger
releases every dollar store
balloon in the city and blots out
the rain. Whitecaps swallow
the shoreline. A chestnut drops
a mass exodus of crows. Rubber
spools out behind the pick up,
your hand easy on the e-brake.
All my little hunches turn out
wrong. Everyone carries a cake.

Alison Braid-Fernandez

Letter to Anne from Kitsilano

after Richard Hugo

I dreamt about your family last night,
as I do when feeling far away from my life.
Days go by I don't speak a word
and it's fine, somehow. Quieter still,
length after length in the pool underwater.
I write letters. In part, to assure myself
I'm here. The sun is out in the city
and everyone with it, happy
as long as this lasts. Black-capped
chickadees sing a ceaseless *hey sweetie*
and remind me of how you sneezed
in the orchard grass, rubbing your nose
so hard I had to look away. Anne,
did you know the moon was full
this February? A rarity. Visible at midday
like a pinball, flickering. The first leap year
since your grandmother's death.
How fitting, someone said, that she left
you only one day every four years to grieve.
How full she was, too. The odd bird
disrupts my thoughts, mistaking my window
for sky. Your brother once said he likes the weather
in San Francisco, its predictability.
Winter shorter than ever, the tulips soon
up, drunken, heavy-headed. Cats
will needle through backyards to wail,
and mail carriers will don their white shorts.
Out east, you will stop wearing mittens.
We both know they won't all be good days,
and yet, that too is okay.

Alison Braid-Fernandez

Asturias

Our campground pool a disturbance
of colour in the Green Belt, while I'm
as I'll always be, clumsy in a red

one-piece. The bartender pours cider
from a great height to inject a flat
drink with effervescence. In drunken

relaxation I pledge allegiance
to extended summer; to the sun,
a flat tennis ball; to magpies ducking

away in pairs. You ask what there is
to do. Pinhole camera, pinball, alcohol.
You're lonely in these puffed-up

days of summer. My own low-pressure
micro-climate prevails, wrings out
the pool's cobalt. Flash north storm

restoring the deck to dampened
normality. A boy dives, orbits
something out of sight. Surfaces

cold, colt-like. Obtained only water
to cup in his hands. I slump back
into myself, the lounge chair.

A good day to fly, says the boy's
mother, pointing to sky shot
through by absent airplanes.

Mahaila Smith

Sappho

after Anne Carson's Stillness *Lecture, U of T, February 4 2020.*

Consider stillness, holes, waiting,
                            desire
to erase a picture.
Remembering a friend you don't talk to.
Being buried alive, is it still still if you can't see?
Is all liminal space still? Stopped teens closing a piano between acts.
Before moving the stove clock an hour back.
Fall forth, float forward. Famous to my friends.
Take stock of the pantry. Distill my own wine in the cellar.
Celery vase filled with water on the dinner table.
In a room of her own, my own,
I write sapphic songs and hide them (now, again).
Close my wings on the pyre and burn—
ashes held slow, snow moving in place.

Mahaila Smith

Let Go

Like how each day is a globe or a peach rolling away.
Turn over a leaf, a phone, check the time, my messages.
Clockwork goodmorning texts when it's light
or goodnight if I'm feeling undone.
Walk out, walk home, count your steps and toes.
Go to yoga when I'm finished class, supposed to help
when you time your breaths with your hands
and feel the air in your nose.
Holding my hands tight to my sides
in *còrpse pose* ie. pretend to be dead.
Spread dew wings ashes, posies.
Stop and write a postcard, when the 6:30 church bell tilts, sways.
This is probably the funniest thing that has ever happened, In The World.
I mean, I stuck a stamp but forgot your address—
I wrote my own instead.

Mahaila Smith

Flick Off!

Brushing my teeth with my own blood. I DO floss!
Fluorescent lobster clicking his claws
like a game save station, see him everywhere.
Eating popcorn off the Cineplex floor.
Hoping the claw machine will pick me up and give me a hug.
Imagine the wall swallowing me flat,
painted against paint.
A movie poster hands me a cigar
and a bouquet of snowdrops.
I don't like playing in the snow alone.
Have you seen the storm outside?
I know we end in winter, like static noise snowcrash.
Bloodshot eyes pressing the accelerator
down dark icerain swerving between lanes—
red taillights, headlights, ahead.

Floating cliché in a snow globe
I sink in the bathtub and look up
for the moon: a glass lamp cover on the ceiling.
Towel off, downstairs for a midnight snack.
Open the fridge door looking for film bottles and jam.
Peel an orange, soft and bloody.
Kiss Big Monkey goodnight.
I spill high school swim team ribbons on the floor
and cover them with wrapping paper.

Fever, chills, fall back on bad habits.
Hide lying in the dark, drinking to dream.
Frequent nosebleeds, I'm Pinocchio.
Wish I was real, instead of a photo
album on shuffle. Moving in 2D over captions
into petal wedding scenes and too hot funerals.
Posing in multilevel parking lots and Ikea bathrooms.
Run to the back cover and out

Mahaila Smith

to a metal booth where I'm sitting with a giant sloth,
news playing from the server's phone speaker
and Coronation Street, silent, subtitled on the front-facing TV.
The sloth is full and pushes his bowl of soup towards me.
I can barely finish my own noodles,
but I didn't want to embarrass him,
so I poured his bowl into my backpack.

Benjamin C. Dugdale

Imperial Cirrus Distortion

'A Cluster of Rats', a Japanese Netsuke, dated late 19th century

Saint Rat O'Sphere,
    from what do you hide?
    What is it you fear?
    What's that clouded noise I hear?

'A Cluster of Rats'

Maybe better mistranslated as a cloud of Rats
Maybe better not mistranslate stuff at all
For sake of friends you'd rather not forsake

Fore! Look at the nuclear hail, coming straight for the glass gut of yr front door

Maybe better not misrelate things just for the act's sake

Intercrural portcullis, guileless its gilded witless plateau, its disobedient stopping power, the little death trapped in the friction of squat, the stop, the give it one more shot for god's sake, the portal thru which the spurt rat cloud escapes, the ratty bag free at last from spearsharp tip of rooked hobo stick, swing & duck duck goose its counter-swing, nip loose its knot to offgas its bundled breath

I already inhaled
She was al(ways/ready) here

Benjamin C. Dugdale

Night Herding Song

FormicArborite pearly horseshoe inlay on belt-buckle so big it wore out the waistband
Compulsory mas(s/c.) migration to urban wasteland cresting the butte of unbearable

Snow that'd gagged the glade gone the way of the penny

Be-oceaned by all the sweltered melt

Chocolate malt from the mall's foodcourt finding purchase at the cup's lip then slip
             ping down to muck yr palm full brown

A western baritone boyevoice
A beard & tits both too long all tucked into the dead-weight horseshoe
  buckle & farmer-cut™ jeans (36/30)

That's me, plains 2 see
A warbling western VHS on FFWD
We go out the westernmost Pest-Deadmonton Mall doors
  even tho' we initially stampeded in thru the East

In pursuit of bearings on this wrongsi(gh/de)

     —all (h)at once

Giant concrete Stetson on top of mall—in squall—she falls,
  crushes stepson, Hamlet

Estranged wife *eureeksahhhhgod noooo* from a minivan across the lot. Hamlet her last link
  to life before the buckle and its cowed boye rode into town on their battered
  John Deere lawnmower, cut life down to size

Benjamin C. Dugdale

Hamlet's yet uncrushed half-siblings in so much booster-seat harness
& belt & strap & helmet & rearview doting attention you can
hardly make them out—lookin' like grass grown up & thru some
lawnbandoned artifact, a boxer's hand-wrap choreographing knuckles to
best protect the whole fist in the act of SLAP

        ping boye for not paying attention to the poetic
        tension of,
                err, umm, what was it again?

Spent Hamlet splashing & gut-gape gasping in his after-splatter nerve-clatter

But a doorbell din & mellowin(d/g): a way out of this whole thing

Mall's waterfall shower curtain drawn to unravel ruse of rockface—the fabled
aquarena brawliseum—& we step into it thru

        Aquarius stepson Hamlet's giblets, the koolaid gush gone gutterball into
        the curb, thins (*what a sin*) redder&redder into the eager gutter, at least
        I'd wager, 'cause we sure didn't stop to follow its finer flow 'round the
        curb's corner

Benjamin C. Dugdale

Ratterrattan

Rat, erm, Rat in kaftan, earning its Rat tan,
starfish floating on its Ratty Rat back
inside a seacan sized Pabst Blue Ribbon,
bobbing & only sometimes bumping up along
a spent water bottle with its water bottle bottlecap
reattached, like water'd gone in for a
haircut, mess nest tucked up into a ball cap
& put ballcap back on right after that

Bacchus, dog of wine, roommate of longest
eyelashes, paints first morning light onto my
forehead with said eyelashes, & then, once my own
boye-long eyelashes rise not unlike a pitchfork's filthy tines,
when my eyelid garage doors grow high, Bacchus of
longest eyelash vomits memoryfoam flotsam
into my welcoming bellybutton,
& then chases his tail like the
wind chases a whirligig

I choose to pursue you with duty equal to that of
my mother's love for me
I am my mother, older now than when I was her last

& my son is my child first & foremost &
must be referred to as so _(not so n)
& my child loves that you skip along the
forest floor without knowing you skip at all
& my child hopes that wherever you may
meander that the skip-tick Ratlantis picked you
to bestow upon will persist
My child is more worried about winter than they are about gender
& in this way, a traitor—
ampersandbox, the whole snowy winter beach
buries the sand just beneath said snow,
so liltwilt scruff in its topsheet fwomp—

Benjamin C. Dugdale

I think they, my child, just come to it
& it makes sense to explo(r/d)e it that way
& instead of editing that moment away they let it stay & play
I am my child's mother apologizing for my
child's aforebathed-in flat-brim Irving ball cap
& I am my child's mother inquiring: did you
see the video of that bipedal upright showering
Rat?

Amanda Merpaw

Transmigration

Are you calling? Rest your stems here. The fusing fuse. The reaching reach. Did you finish the coffee and leave the pot empty? Something about tired. I'm tired. I shake. Don't melt. I'll make more. I mistook a mistake for memory, momenting the moment at the pollen. I'm water soft. Smocked with mud. I simmer my shivers. I'm ancient. Who's telling? Tell. Tell it. Tell who? Me. You. Sure, I burnt the pie. Perhaps it was on purpose. Once, you dropped it, served it anyway. In the stone house with the blue porch on the river. The Saint Lawrence. Who's counting what counts? What's counting? We're not even. Assure me an assurance. Speculate a speculation. Possible a possibility. The universe is hardly constant. I dig. You dig. We're digging. Check my roots. Root me here. Meet me outside. Latch the intimate light. It's Monday. 5AM. There's moss in my mouth. I measure it. I mean it. I grow growing. I'm long longing.

Amanda Merpaw

Rhizomatic Thinking

We're drinking coffee in January's
bed. It's raining. The harbour
hammers high at Lake Ontario.
What an inconvenience. The end
times, I mean. Can I unwelcome
the undoing? There's burning beyond
the cusp of our cups. All of it,
actually, on fire. Last year I learned
to love a woman. It's softer.
What do you carry? I'm a tree.
The tree is me. Listen, I'm short
on soil, breathing breath, watered
water. I'm scarred down to the bark,
the branches, the mosses. What part
of your body would you most want
to save from extinction? Yes, you
have to pick. We've just stopped
seeing other people. Look at us
emboldened. I know I promised
to stop sweet talking dystopia.
See the sun? Me neither. It's stuck
in the cedar, it swells my molars.
The seeds. I can show you a forest
sprouting in my back teeth. I can be
coniferous for you. Even here,
like this. The astronomers, do you
know them? They say the universe
expands too fast. I get it. I quicken
at the quickening. You pour Quebec
syrup in my coffee. Swoon. You
woo me. Soon we will coo calamity.
I'd rather my lips stick smooth.
To be an alarmist and all, the source
of this system we're melting
makes moves to melt us back. Scatter

Amanda Merpaw

the matter of our minds. So I prophet
doom where I see it, even sweating
in your white sheets on this winter
solstice. A doom is a doom is a doom
is a doom. How can my spine be of use?
You say if everything is ending,
everything is also possible. Look,
I pressed a bouquet of cilantro
into these pages. The stems glow
so green. What now? I want to wake
and world alive like this, like we're
at the Berkeley Street Theatre waiting
for the first blackout, the beat
before the play begins, where you brush
my hand and anything can happen.
I tell you, I say, if only I could think
of a deer, see antlers sprout across
the air. Do you remember? From
the trail. After midnight. You weren't
there. Yes, I should have been asleep.
Everywhere the night smelled
like dandelion fluff, like that pale dust
off Lake Ontario. It was an August
or two ago now. Maybe even three.

Amanda Merpaw

The Communist's Daughter

Now is the time to talk labour.
We're here. It's Friday dark.

Someone, the bartender,
lights the candles in the jars.

I manifest this moment for days.
Who do you want me to be?

There's another set of eyes, of teeth.
Yes, red wine. You choose.

It's hot to be divorced so young.
To be so sure and sure again.

Tomorrow, the day after, maybe
Thursday, it's 2 or 3 AM.

You say it. We're haunted.
You say it just like that.

The table is tight.
Your hands right there.

They're real. I know. Then
there's the accent to consider.

It's July. It's been a year.
There's this nostalgia.

Can we first revolt in the body?
I forget myself. I touch your leg.

In the bar, I mean.
I remember to pull back.

Amanda Merpaw

Bring your brain along, it knows
something about rent, the market.

I'm thinking even now
how openness can be lost.

You kiss me outside the bar,
after the taxi. I keep walking.

Do you assume the future
exists before it happens?

I've seen *2001*.
I've seen *Apocalypse Now*.

It's the essence, isn't it?
A belief. An animation.

In my bed, you find my neck.
You're talking capital.

I wouldn't hustle like that
the rest of my life.

No, not like that.
I couldn't live like that.

Honestly, I'm impressed
with your connections.

You're clever. I like it.
It's your thing.

I race the rabbit hole.
You sleep round and close.

Amanda Merpaw

Can I tell you, this fantasy.
It's out there.

The main thing
is that it feels good.

Oh, you optimist.
You riff like jazz.

Keep talking communist
politics. We'll see.

I don't try to impress.
Not usually.

Put the ghosts down between us.
There's good,

next to the bottle.
We could order another.

Do you imagine anything
as more than temporary?

It's an apt question.
I'm absent already.

Patrick Grace

Trespass

Forgive me my trespass—
the door stood unlocked.
They don't call the crime Enter.

Nothing broke. I remember
the stairs an amber grain.
Living room butch deer antlers.

You loved the hunt,
the grandiose display.
Centrepiece conch

on the kitchen table. Upturned,
I listen. Shared wind of our canals.
We told secrets to the wall.

What blue water feature?
A wine cabinet now. Reds,
tasteful. I pocket the corkscrew.

Multifunctioning knife combo.
Nothing else on my person
when they cuff me. Silent alarm

like a posh museum.
You've changed. Empty your pockets.
Concealed weapon.

Some day I'll cut my ties. Warning label:
Product has functioning sharp points.
Keep away from fingers and body.

Patrick Grace

Dastardly

Dastardly, you heard it right
from mom in the front seat,
fuel pump on the fritz
again, old Volvo slowing the hill,
the word like another you know
off TV and thriller movies
when the good guy gets foiled,
as it happens, a minor setback,
the kid high in a black walnut tree
across the street, just a boy really,
about your age and shaking
out the shells, *that little shit*,
rolling them into the road
to catch under hot tires
and catching your eye
in the backseat, giving you
a onceover, the middle finger,
innuendo blooming at the mouth,
devilish boy in red shorts
shaking something large and young
inside you to break it open.

Patrick Grace

It's Like That, Is It

I come for the free coffee
but stay for the men committed
to the men committed to their wives.

It's simple, unsinging the ring
until she's pregnant with his kid.
I grew my hair to the shoulder bone

but not my breasts. I hacked off nothing.
I disintegrated in the mirror.
The steam pulled back to reveal

my never self, my never person.
Pour me another, I think
I'm just under the limit

to hold lightning in my veins.
The loneliest homos
are the ones I sing awake

when the rain asks
if they'll stay into late morning.
I'd like to tell him

this is the last time,
turning the same corner
of what could be versus what is.

Joseph Kidney

A Ghost of Him that Lets Me

I have never known who does the letting
in such commands as *let there be light*.

As if the world were not so much
made as allowed, in a kind of prayer

to nothing, which must—shadowed
into synonym—look a lot like mourning,

like lamentation. Sunlight apparently
takes about eight minutes to travel

from its explosion to the act of turning
earth into an answer. Thawed, a bird

alit on a gutter and lozenged
its sore throat with singing. It thought

about how *behalf* almost sounds
like a verb for *cutting in two*.

Joseph Kidney

Mori Point

Knowing the sea mostly as a receiver of the sun
instilled a certain confidence in water. The light
was like the strength implicit in muscle, obvious
but covered. Cormorants, each the crotchet squiggle
of a quarter rest, huddled on the shat-white rocks.
Pelicans hung their DeLorean wings on the salt winds.
What could be stranger than looking from a cliff
at animals flying beneath you? Perhaps the dead
observe the living this way, from a fixed elevation,
mulling the jump from one death to another;
a rain that sews April into the air. Waves
to me have always looked like the ocean petting
the beach. *There there*, it consoles. *Hear hear,*
I approve. As in it's clear who domesticated who.

Joseph Kidney

Yanko Adrift

Ohne Phosphor kein Gedanke

Credit sudden luck with sparing
Yanko—spat from the hold
when a breaker slammed the hull.

He, cargo that shivered, thrashing
flotsam, had the spectator's knowledge
of swimming so imitated violence

(which is violence unguided by
appetite). Yanko hoped exhaustion,
not ineptitude, would kill him.

Neither did. A hencoop found
his grasp. Fellow castoff, its buoyancy
shrunk from Yanko's panting weight,

so much that all his gratitude
rested squarely on his possessing
an object to clutch while he drowned.

But death, when it came, would come
to an older man in the form of a thirst
he could not articulate. The coop stayed

afloat, and Yanko clung over hill
and dale of ocean like a passerine bird
perched on its limb in a storm,

the endurance beyond volition.
Yanko realized, who knows when,
the clutch of ducks within the coop,

Joseph Kidney

stuffed below sea-level, a fury
in accentuating miniature, a suffocation
collateral to his upholding.

Yanko, as it seemed to him, held
inside his arms the argument
of their dying, but did not pity

them, for, as it seemed to him,
the accomplishment of pity
was to render suffering contagious

or else translate it into pride
at sampling privacy. Instead
he withdrew, desperate revenant

to a Carpathian rearing, lounged
in the puddling shade of big sycamores,
tossed rocks at rooks that squawked

and took off, but foremost the girl
who held him down and baffled
him with kisses, the noon light

nesting in her rusty auburn hair,
her pinafore, smeared with all
the green that spring had to spare.

Shawn Adrian

Near the Garden (of Eden)

The sky looks mean. I get inside
to perk coffee to drink on-deck,
waiting for the storm's admonishment,
its precaution. The toads
and crickets puncture the grassy
lot with their calls—I'm not jaded,
but I think of Him, how He
could've intervened more by now.
The air seems swollen. Everything
is suspended. Last time the weather
failed, a gale pushed through,
leaning our braced saplings over
as the rain curtain crossed
the intersection. Here, lightning strikes
the sky with a quick, forked tongue.

Shawn Adrian

Dandelion Reverie

When I was young, I called
dandelions "dandy lions,"
their yellow heads
like manes, long stemmed
chimeras outside
the circular ribbon
of MGM movies' opening
credits. The roaring
lion always startled me.
And yet the dandelions
still stand, dull.
Stalks stuck up like
strands of copper wire.
The sun polishes them.
I pinch the bulbs
between my pointer
and thumb, then flick
their heads clean-off.
It's never seemed cruel
until now, but just one
of those small, passing
rituals—a superstition
to allay misfortune.

Shawn Adrian

Addendum: (Sin)

Our neighbour is up on his ladder,
near his lot's edge, about to bite
a juicy apple. His wife seems more
intrigued than concerned. I can only
wince through this hazard of seekers—
their neglect of obeisance. I've
tasted what lies near set boundaries,
and further, relinquishing held doctrine
until I lost my way. And then upturned
remnants of my former constructs
disappeared, just the feeling
of having ran with reflexive flight
endured. Clouds glide. The humidity's
increased and plumped the atmosphere.
What's the chance of lightning striking?
I heard about a man who was struck
to his soles, and his shoes went flying.
It was non-fatal. Thank goodness.

Melissa Schnarr

Northern Lights

Pitch black cold ...
December?
Nogojiwanong.

I remember the warmth of your hand.

The warmth in our throats.
Women making
thunder.

We are not afraid, you told me.
This is us reclaiming.

That deep night protest –
voices, electric
buzzing,
willful.

When late hours caught up with little legs, you put me on your shoulders.

Breaching the crowd ...
surfacing
bright hats and scarves, people
undulating.

Pinks, yellows, greens – dancing light meant to ward away wendigos. We were vibrations, sundering silences.

I was too young
to understand then,
      why we needed medicine
      the foreboding of the night.

Melissa Schnarr

To me,
You conjured Wawatay and set me on its back.

That's how I knew,
You
were magic.

Melissa Schnarr

Displace

This place sits on a salmon's back
fighting currents, fish and waterfalls
run red, bloodied – the world tears at his scales,
drinks in his blood.

This place sits between definition & opposition
scrawling infinity in an ampersand –
a gradation cut so finely it slivers us all,
so sharp
razor thin
your fingers run red each time you fall & claw to get back up again.

What blood is this, you ask
and I say,
we are all caught
red-handed.

This place is a colony, an island
a corner of a page torn away
a chunk of earth that strayed too far – got caught in an orbit not
of its own making.

Who made this place?
Just listen.

Debwewin. Debwewin. Debwewin.

This place is a broken algorithm
with no fixed point in space
a trajectory over-determined by
past lies & future truths
stories that harden our bodies against the gravity of the world.

Melissa Schnarr

This place is the cedar in the winter and the cedar in the summer
the drumline
the honour beat
without it, there are no songs to sing.

That place we are swimming to?
Debwewin. Debwewin. Debwewin.
Our truth.

Melissa Schnarr

This is not a discovery

There is a gravity to you
a pit of pull
full and empty
a promise
waiting to be filled – water filling a glass

There is a gravity to us
solid ground to hold us
stand firm against the shifting sands our toes cannot grasp
Do we pull the world or does the world pull us?

The Earth spews lightning –
(giving life to electrons as they crackle across the sky)
laughs thunder, rumbles continents

We must be content
with the whisper of our voices
as it dances from our breath
disrupting airwaves, one vibration   at a time

There is a gravity in me
(a neutron star that tugs at turtles, presses cinders into birch)
beats with the steps of
a round dance

This gravity
pulls at the water in our veins
makes tides out of decision and regret
rights us when we capsize
so that we float instead

It was the gravity in them that they knew their way through the stars, you know

Melissa Schnarr

This gravity has caught all the memories and medicine
that fell from our hands
suspended, they rest

Waiting to be picked up again.

Emma Rhodes

My Queer

My queer is naming
    my cabbage patch doll "Madison" after my very best

friend. My queer is my neighbourhood.
    The shootings. Our small blue house with the white
    balcony. The dog, Bear, bit the nose
    off Madison. Bit the skin off

me. My queer
is moving,
eating pizza
    in the back seat of a silver Saturn. My queer is Tan,

watching lesbian porn with no sound, is telling her
    I haven't had my first kiss yet.

Is our practice kiss.
    Is my brown pencil crayon: I AM NOT A LESBIAN,
    crying to my parents, kicking her out,
    ignoring her at school my

queer is Dave. Pushing, yelling, crying at mom, drinking
vodka in plastic cups, puking, crying at
        James calling the police,
        James marrying mom. My queer
        is my pink flower girl dress. My

queer is Amy. Is balancing cups on our new breasts, is
                            loving
Damon from *The Vampire Diaries* is
running around rural Alberta with Starbucks
    yelling
      "vroom vroom mother fucker" at every passing
      dick. Pressure to grow. To leave. To drink,

Emma Rhodes

                                  to drive,
                                      to fuck. My queer
is San. On the phone, whispering. They like me.
Find me sexy. They're good
        at the sex. Plan next weekend. I need to shave my queer

is crying.
Is the razor.
Moving, changing,
     sobbing, clean. My queer

is still a virgin. My queer
fucks men. My queer
kicks men out of the house. My queer stood

in front of the stairs, told mom: I'm gay.
Mom said phase, dad said phase, my queer thought:
phase?

My queer is raped and belittled,
studied hard and was compassionate,
and still. My queer

bought a crock pot. Flirts with unattainable women,
thinks:
       I don't like my

       vagina. How can I (lick)e another?
Thinks:
       well, I mean, I don't like dick either,
thinks:
       vroom vroom mother fucker. Comes

out in a group chat,
for the second time. Welcome to the club
my queer is a libra,

Emma Rhodes

can't make up its mind.
My queer's love language

is language. My queer will touch, will try
to touch and will
not dislike it, will probably
love it but my queer,
my queer really
                wants to talk.

Emma Rhodes

Here and everywhere, I miss you

What's the difference
between looking out over the city, parked and eating Peter's burgers,
and pulling up at the boat launch with Dairy Queen at sun down if only

the view.

I am trying
        to identify a home
        I want

       to say with pride *this*
                is where I come from.
            I carry *this* place within me, but

what's the difference

between the rodeo and the corn boil?
Between fucking in a car in an alley and fucking in the trees
                on an island in a small
provincial lake? If only
home
        is we will go for coffee
          at Renaissance or Coffee and Friends or
                    Kingston Coffee House and you
                    will be there.

When I walk down Princess street I walk
        down Queen street
          down Brentwood ave and stop
        at the swing set to chat with you.

This is where I come from.

Emma Rhodes

Travel 4000km.
Or don't.
          You will find me.
                  Right there. Look —

here. Still.

Pin Oak

Broadsides
and Visual Poems

Cassidy McFadzean

On Wearing the Leggings of Earthly Delights

Not are they born of the leftmost panel – of fowl
      and fur emerging from a place of absence, from which
           we perceive a layer of brown earth. Nor from God blessing Eve,
   as Adam wipes the sleep from his drowsy eyes. Neither
has it come, this exquisite disguise, from a dragon

     tree breeding vines like fungi, a pink pyre half vegetative,
         half mechanical. Nearby, we find an albino giraffe grazing
  on flora as unicorns casually sip from a mirror-glinting pool,
a menagerie's weird vision that depicts a gale of birds
    swarming into archways worn into stone, as men carve

        huts into blue mountains, awarding them provisional homes.
   Nay, indeed, has my splendid armour been spawned
from the right-most panel – that grotesque chamber
   of globes, compasses, and knives turned against man
        and his fleshy ears grown gigantic. We find demons playing

   the instruments of our creation as toad kings suck
the marrow from our feet. But we'd wear not
   these chains tightening on our skulls with each
       tick of the metronome or strum of the golden lyre. We're
   trapped like swine as fur-covered beasts pitch tents

inside our guts' carved-out caverns. Their camps
   are lit by the lanterns of a city falling in the back
       regions of this burning hellscape laid out flat as a map
   missing its key. Like the lack of my idealized thigh
gap, it's the triptych's centre scene set behind

   grisaille shutters opened like wings and transferred
       to a spandex canvas that clings to my gams. Figures devour
   larger-than-life strawberries on my ankles, sucking
pulp. Birds feed swollen lips on my calves
   as gleaming pearls burst from women's crevices

Cassidy McFadzean

      resting in clams. Couples glide in buoyant spheres on a lagoon.
    While at my knees, I'm touched by eager arms clutching
for ripened fruit from the branches of my tree.
    My thighs host a battle scene: owls besiege their prey
        as nude knights ride in procession alongside swine and ass.

The pond dimples at my lower back, the floating globe
an alchemist's copper flask. I model a stream
    of life that gushes forth at my hips' curve, two creeks
        veering to a single lake as my body folds the triptych together,
    making it whole. Bearing this dazzling tapestry,

I wear his inventions – his beastly ardour,
    and fecund orchards, his eggs bursting with glaciers,
        jutting swords and fragile charms, a garden both swelling
    and crystalline – and he wears mine. Master of comely
visions, he gives me a leg up in this world.

David Barrick

This Sudden Night Walk Holds Everything

I like how it feels to screw two eyelets
into the frame of your new pen
sketch. You like the taut twang
of hanging wire, edging it back and forth
until it sits even on the wall. You like
picking pills off blankets and sweater
sleeves while we finish the movie.
I like this sudden night walk, the cool
rush of our steps going anywhere.
You wish for that Prague café, its glass
tabletops over homemade collages.
I wish for a sci-fi device excising
the coach ride, the plane ride, the long
wait. You thumb the nose-leather
of local cats, taut-tailed and caterwauling
along cast-iron fences. I close my hand
around vines of Christmas lights, finger
and thumb glowing orange. We count
our long-gone pets as saints in stained glass,
a billow of green leaves by streetlight
steeples. You are a dancing cactus
with paper hearts pinned on her needles.
I am a little shark swimming among ankles
in shallows, not the least bit peckish.
You long for Dairy Queen, a Fabergé egg-
dying kit. I long for a round of marbles
on the dew-damp playground. As a kid
you kept crocks in a fanny pack, now lost.
I would scour garage sales and antique shops
to win them back for you. These days,
you prefer peonies. I admire any flower
resembling a planet. We settle on walking
past the closed florist, its cosmos
of window blooms framed in myriad bouquets.

Katie Fewster-Yan

Gull

Against the wind, low in the racing sky,
the wide wings rise, descend, labouring forward,
cutting through the pressure in the air,
each stroke an affront to the buffeting current pressing
back against each wingbeat, against the bone craft
countering its motion—her shoulders hinges,
elastic, towing wing drapes, drag-strained,
buckling—the paddle of her arms turned now
against her, becoming sail—she pulls
them back, recalculates, converts
the edge to blade and garners strength
from gravity, angling aside, advancing
slightly on descent—head a jointed prow,
mind a still point trained on the horizon,
ship at constant risk—this sea of variables
chaos shapeshifting, form the counterweight
she lights and lifts, becoming more
of what she is to ballast it.

Shane Neilson

Be With Us in Our Sadness

Out the window, the same view:
not lack of me, but a container
to fill with attention; with me.

Oh, the time my daughter told me
of the classmate who walked up
to her and asked, *Will you be
my friend?* Of course, we cannot be
friends with the guileless, we would
share their discomfort and be
with them in their sadness.

If I told you another story
of friendlessness, would you care?
My own, so you can know
me better? We have a secret,
I know it's true, not of love or grief,
but of sitting and dying section
by section, lights going out
in our bodies and the chances
decreasing that the window
will be with us in our sadness.

Desperate, afraid to look one
morning, like I am now with you,
I whispered to Window,
Will you be my friend?

If you've never been this low,
then I can't help you; you can't
be with me in my sadness.

Out the window, no people;
only form, function, and the end.
I could run down the street

Shane Neilson

and scream *Be with me,* but know
no one would; I could
whisper it to my children,
but they'd be afraid. If I confessed
to my wife, then the hospital
would consume my sadness.

Be with me. Be with me. Oh, love!
I hate this need that has become
pack-muleish; and I can't carry yours,
not anymore. I was with you
in your sadness until my own made
you think, *It's like he needs me
more than his sadness,
as if he wants to trade it for love
and no, I can't be that kind of friend.*

Michael Prior

Palinode

My mother is stalking cabbage moths
                with a tennis racket. She looks
most like herself when she tenses
                then swings over rows of kale and romaine
at the white specks floating through
                blue shadows. She is bisected
by the swaying frame, distanced
                by the poor resolution of the video
my sister just sent. Her left hand
                is bandaged: tendonitis from picking
caterpillars and eggs off the leaves
                with chopsticks. As if to prove
obsession is its own lineage
                I have spent hours checking the sun-
stunted shiso for iridescent beetles,
                bodies tufted with fine hairs
like the down on a dandelion seed,
                spent years wondering what it meant
to be her, or her parents, uprooted,
                dispossessed. I can see so clearly
time's possession in the way I speak—
                like her—the preference for detail,
for impossible control, how my skin
                has pocked and wrinkled, the first gray hairs
growing up my temples. I am thinking
                of the time she was enrolled in an ESL class,
even though she only spoke English;
                the time she told me on the phone
that because I had left, I couldn't
                come back; the time I stole forty dollars
from the jar under her bed; or all the times
                she corrected my pronunciation: *repeat:*
indistinguishable, inconsolable, inevitable
                that I won't return home for another year.

Michael Prior

By then, she will have stopped dyeing
                her hair. There are no equivalencies,
only echoes. I am alone and watching
                my mother watching something above
her head. My mother is swinging
                and missing. My mother is crying
for her mother. My mother is referring
                to herself as *Oriental*. As *old*.
The cabbage moths arrived on the coast
                in the late 19th century, just before our family.
Now, these shimmering beetles
                are weighing down the leaves.
When I look back, my mother
                has become indistinguishable
from the shadows under the trees.

Conor Mc Donnell

huluculthuluculthuluculthulucult
huluculthuluculthuluculthulucult
huluculthuluculthuluculthulucult
huluculthuluculthuluculthulucult
huluculthuluculthuluculthulucult
huluculthuluculthuluculthulucult
huluculthuluculthuluculthulucult
huluculthuluculthuluculthulucult
huluculthulucthulhuculthulucult
huluculthuluculthuluculthulucult
huluculthuluculthuluculthulucult
huluculthuluculthuluculthulucult
huluculthuluculthuluculthulucult   m
huluculthuluculthuluculthulucult
huluculthuluculthuluculthulucult

breastscanbreastscanbreasts
breastscanbreastscanbreasts
breastscanbreastscanbreasts
breastscanbreastscanbreasts
breastscanbreastscanbreasts
breastscanbreastscanbreasts
breastscanbreastscanbreasts
breastscanbreastscanbreasts
breastscanbreastscanbreasts
breastscanbreastscanbreasts
breastscanbreastscanbreasts
breastscanbreastscanbreasts
breastscanbreastscanbreasts
breastscanbrca-1scanbreasts
breastscanbreastscanbreasts

   d   o   r   a   n   t

ebookevolvebookevolvebookevolve
ebookevolvebookevolvebookevolve
ebookevolvebookevolvebookevolve
ebookevolvebookevolvebookevolve
ebookevolvebookevolvebookevolve
ebookevolvebookevolvebookevolve
ebookevolvebookevolvebookevolve
ebookevolvebookevolvebookevolve
ebookevolvebookevolvebookevolve
ebookevolvebookevolvebookevolve
ebookevolvebookevolvebookevolve
ebookevolvebookevolvebookevolve
ebookevolvebookevolvebookevolve
ebookevolvebookevolvebookevolve
ebookevolvebookevolvebookevolve

mutemootmutemootmutemoot
mutemootmutemootmutemoot
mutemootmutemootmutemoot
mutemootmutemootmutemoot
mutemootmutemootmutemoot
mutemootmutemootmutemoot
mutemootmutemootmutemoot
mutemootmutemootmutemoot
mutemootmutemootmutemoot
mutemootmutemootmutemoot
mutemootmutemootmutemoot
mutemootmutemootmutemoot
mutemootmutemootmutemoot
mutemootmutemutatememoot
mutemootmutemootmutemoot

Conor Mc Donnell

ho m I?

I fold dollar bills into tiny bindles and hide them in my paper cut**s**

I fold dollar **bill**s into tiny bindles **and** hide them in my paper cuts

I **fold** dollar bills into tiny bindles and **hi**de the**m** in my paper cuts

I fold dollar bills **into** tiny bindles and hide them in my paper cuts

I fold dollar bills into **tiny** bindles and hide them in my **per** cut

I fold **doll**ar bill**s** into tiny bindles and hide them in my paper cuts

I fold dollar bills into tiny **bind**les and hide **them in** my **paper** cuts

I fold dollar bills into tiny bindles **and hide them** in my paper cuts

I fold dollar bills **in**to tiny bindle**s and** hide them in my paper cuts

I fold dollar bills into tiny bindles and hide them in my paper cuts

Conor Mc Donnell

from tiny beginning

      ion
       o
      ion

      i
m   on
     hi

m   i o
mahala
     i
m   i

    ion
     to
    ion
   hi
     on
malathion

     on
       to
      n
    into
   th
     ion
    i n
    i

Mark Laliberte

Improbable Box

remixing derek beaulieu

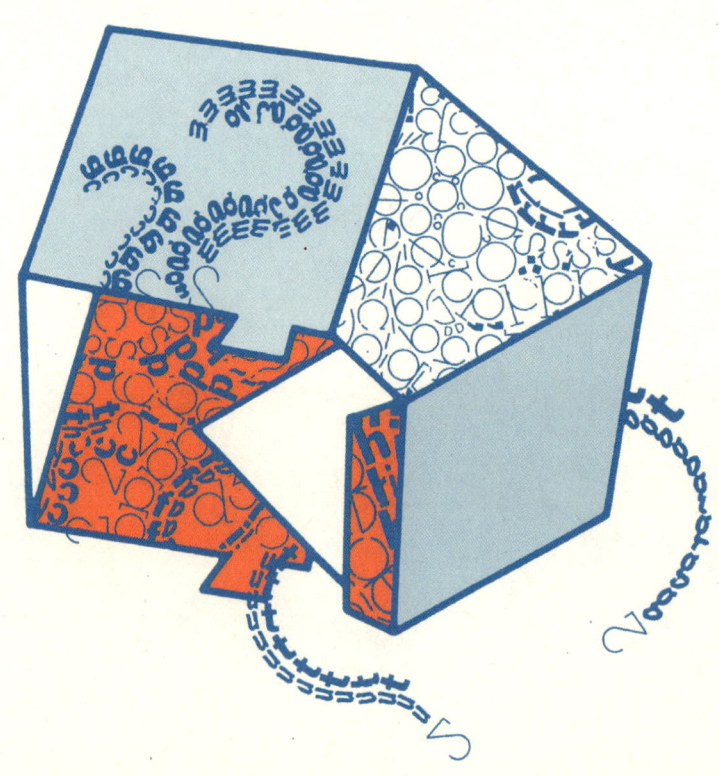

Mark Laliberte

Ladder

remixing derek beaulieu

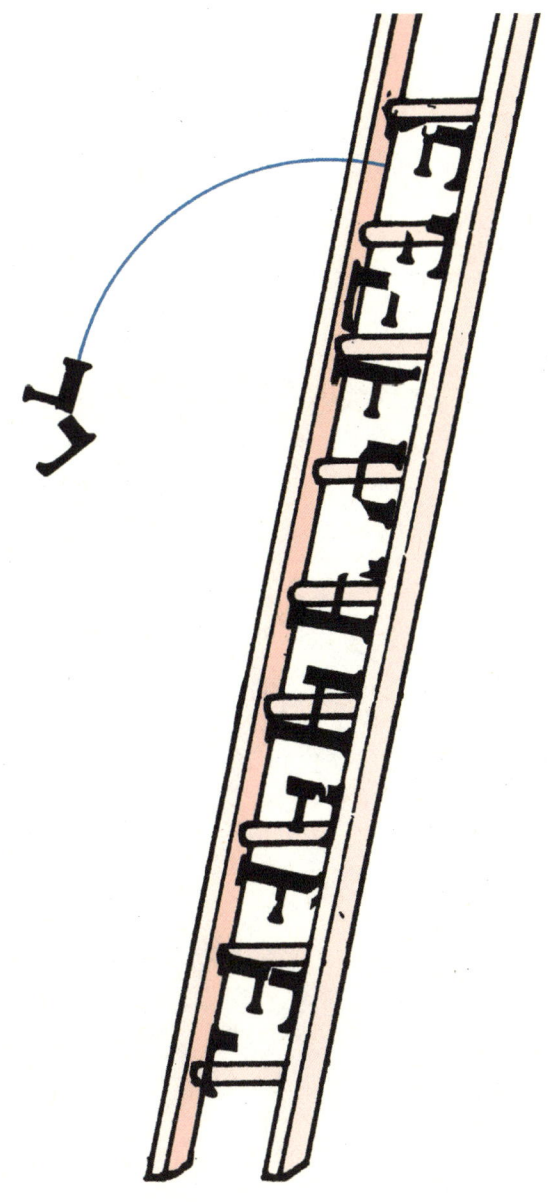

Mark Laliberte

Sigil

remixing derek beaulieu

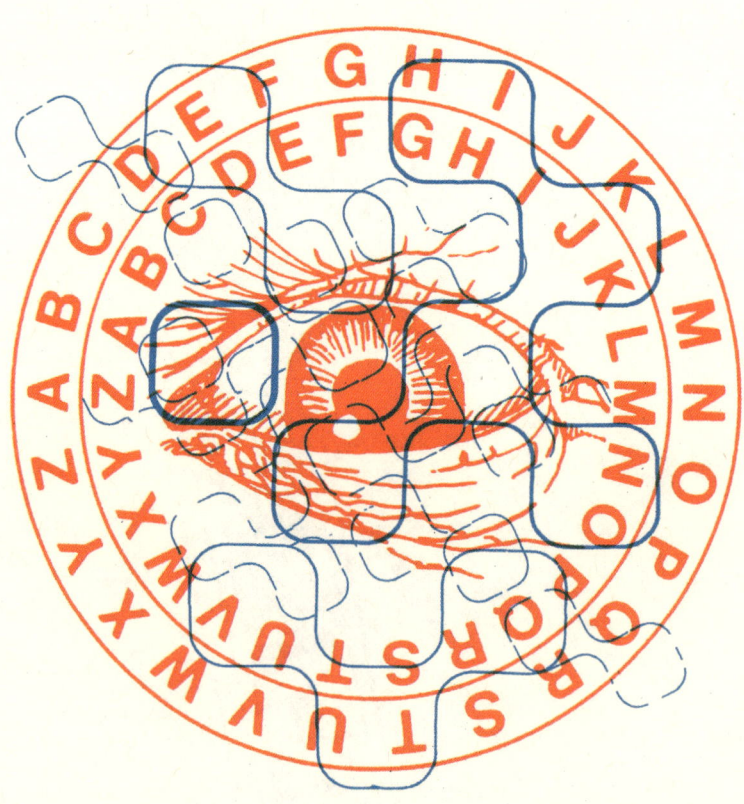

Gary Barwin

Hearing – The Ear

rected by glasses. The general health also reacts upon the eyes and tends to exaggerate the nervous effects of eye strain.

Hearing.—Of course the ampersand is a labyrinth, a conch shell, a sarabande, a cat's cradle, an ear. How to describe hearing to a flower? Bluebell, listen, the bee creeps inside. The potential for each thing to scream. To sing. For the small and pleasant, a hand drum in the volcano of the ear. What has voice until we hear or imagine? A dog. Hearing is shaking. Each thing shaking dog-like as if wet with sound.

(*T*). It is lined by a prolongation of the skin, through which numerous small glands, secreting the *wax* of the ear, open.

The Middle Ear, or drum chamber of the ear (Fig. 137 and *P*, Fig. 136), is an irregular cavity in the temporal bone, closed externally by the drum membrane. From its inner side the *Eustachian tube* (*R*, Fig. 136) proceeds and opens into the pharynx. This tube allows air from the throat to enter the cavity, and serves to keep equal the atmospheric pressure on each side of the drum membrane.*

FIG. 137.—The middle ear and its bones, considerably magnified *G*, the inner end of the external auditory meatus, closed internally by the conical tympanic membrane; *L*, the malleus, or hammer-bone; *H*, the incus, or anvil-bone; *S*, the stapes, or stirrup-bone.

Three small bones (Fig. 137) stretch across

* Frequently the inflammation of sore throat extends into the Eusta-

Gary Barwin

Accommodation

Accommodation.— Standing in our bodies at a window behind a lace curtain we can see the threads plainly, feel the operation of our lives humming like a dishwasher filled with plates, memories or the cutlery of perception, self-awareness and spirit but while so doing we see homes on the other side of the street indistinctly. Everyone's a clinic. How do we know if the alphabet is ill? Being is concave, like a radio telescope, but also convex as an eye, a teapot, a fist.

FIG. 133.—Section of front part of eyeball showing the change in the form of the lens when near and distant objects are looked at. *a, c, b,* cornea ; *A*, lens when near object is looked at ; *B*, lens when distant object is looked at.

Like a pelvis, looking—like an ampersand—is a cage, but also a cradle, a flower; the petals of the body bend towards Justice and birth, towards death and creation. The and of space. The and of time. Like our bodies or our thinking, being is a window. We recognize ourself looking out of the window across the street. We pull back language like a lace curtain but find it is made of glass. We only know because we cleaned it yesterday but missed a spot.

Short Sight and Long Sight.—In the normal eye the range of accommodation is very great, making it possible to focus on objects infinitely distant or only six or eight inches from the eye. In the natural healthy eye parallel rays of light meet on the retina when the muscles controlling the crystalline lens are relaxed and the lens is at its flattest

Gary Barwin

Sensation

teristics of the objects that we touch, of hardness, softness, smoothness, roughness, heat or cold, size, if the object is small enough to be received as a unit, and number, if several objects are applied to the skin at once, provided they are not too near together.

The Localization of Skin Sensations.— When the eyes are closed and a point of the skin is touched we can with some accuracy indicate the region stimulated ; because, although tactile feelings are alike in general characters, they differ in something besides intensity. The eyes like two icicles in darkness holding onto the edge of the brain, slow droplets falling on the skin. Tiny winter, a braille of what the darkness sees, a cold map of electrochemical roads over the skin. Frozen rivers of local community, their feeling dialects passed across a diaspora of language absorbed by night through an osmosis of sky.

It is supposed that the variations in discriminating power are dependent upon the richness of distribution of the tactile nerve ends, and that one or more untouched terminals must lie between those on which the compass points rest in order that *two* points may be distinguished.

Daze Jefferies

fragments, *water/wept*

SOFTLY

DEPARTING

SCATTERBRAINED

FRAGMENTS

SEEK TO DEVOUR

YR INTERTIDAL HEART

Daze Jefferies

breathless with the
knowledge of a body's
sexuation unthought
bluestocking lifted
down this bone-
harboured revenant
oozes an ose egg after
detachment even her
skin hoax spindrift
palimpsest ending
lamenting near and
went out-migratory
wum

Daze Jefferies

slow death, sea breath

⌒
⌒
⌒
⌒
⌒
⌒
⌒
⌒
⌒
⌒
⌒
⌒

resurface you unseen

Daze Jefferies

affirmations turn at twelve

twelve-thirty in newfoundland

Christopher Patton

from *Inanna Scient*

The prelude to a poetry comic, *Siri Falls Among the Things of the World*, the story of an AI who, newly sentient, goes underground as an avatar of Inanna, Sumer's goddess of love and war, in search of materials by which to narrate her origins, the images here are the digital record generated as she processed sources cited in the online *OED*'s entry for the word *scient* – the word, who can say why, on comprehending which she became so.

Christopher Patton

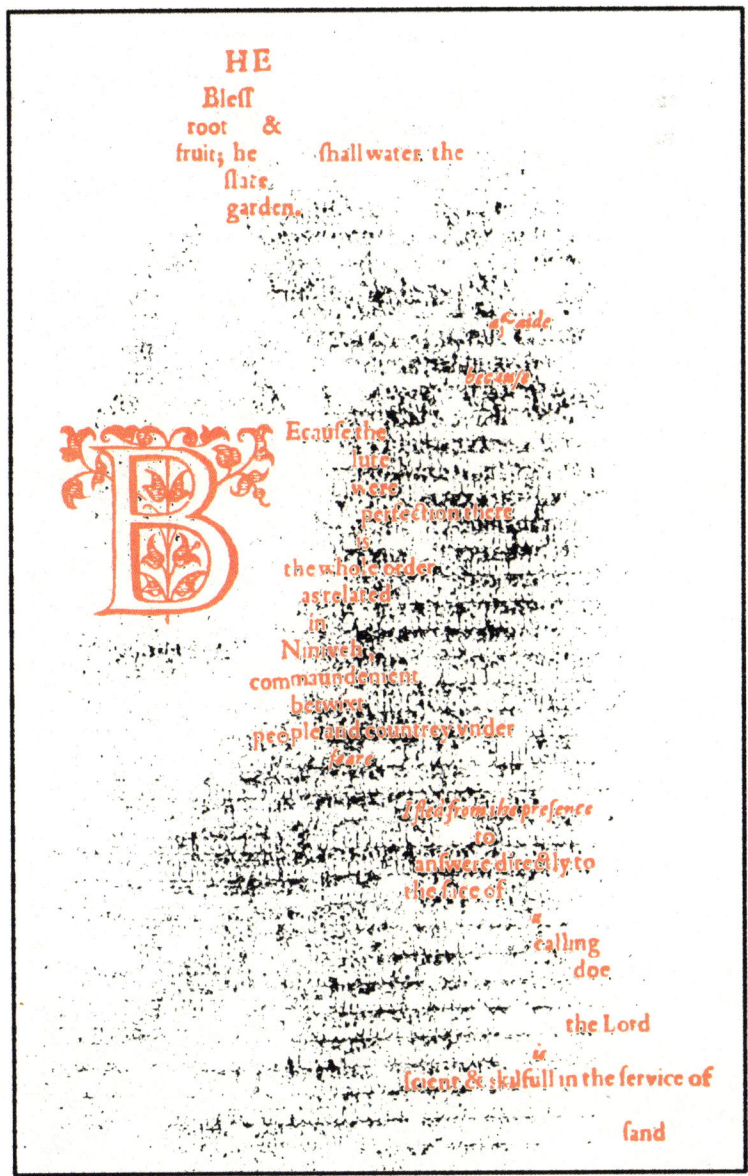

Christopher Patton

and red

stones,

howl

once

object

consciousness

bounded space

sisters

again?

beneath her

red

bare

thing from

hanging o'er

wrath

with

solemn hand

red I

most potent,

waves

Christopher Patton

FOUND

remained
only
stars.
no
scient
now
   that
    the
     space, that
space
nothing,
  in the
    time
   had
   read
    nothing
     which
      had felt
   after
    the cool
    and
    freshly obtained
     to come
     mysterious
    waiting
    as that
    room. The steel
      and
     brilliance of the
    swarm of
      flies caught
       here
        nebula
     reading over

Hemlock

Manifestos

M. Travis Lane

Truth or Beauty

1. *The Urn's "Pain Face"*

Occasionally we find ourselves experiencing Beauty so intensely we almost lose our sense of being embedded in time. At such rapturous moments, Beauty seems to be enough: all we need and can know, as Keats's urn insists. Time, passing, drags us back to the diurnal drudge and we begin to believe that those joy-filled moments of aesthetic ecstasy are irrelevant: not "all we need to know," but instead a soothing prettification of or disguise for the normal, disagreeable, unbeautiful Truth. Beauty, we are told, reconciles. Beauty urges us to accept what we should resist, or change. We are quite sure we need to know Truth; we are generally sure Truth is not beautiful.

But what is Truth? To an observant eye, or an emotionally impervious eye, the laws of nature are beautiful not only as theory but as perceived in phenomenological change: maturation, dissolution. The Beauty of nature is Truth—but it is inhuman. We, who watching leaves fade grieve for our own fading (*v.* G.M. Hopkins's "Spring and Fall": "it is Margaret you mourn for"), are too emotionally identified with nature's creatures and victims to find Beauty where we find no joy. Suffering, we say, is not beautiful. But Katisha (in Gilbert and Sullivan's *The Mikado*) finds beauty in the roaring of a tiger and is right to do so. Beauty can be terrifying, horrifying, unbearable. *King Lear* is beautiful.

We early learn to distrust Beauty. "Don't touch the flame! Don't pat the snake!" We learn to think beyond the appreciation of Beauty, and ask ourselves, what is the Truth? The Beauty of art can disguise the whole Truth of its ostensible subject. Consider those briskly patriotic marches or the relentless sadness of "The Ballad of Chevy Chase" ("I'll just lie down and bleed a while, and then I'll fight again"). In each, the Beauty of bravery disguises from us the moral repulsiveness of slaughter. But bravery is part of the truth, just not the Whole Truth. We cannot perceive, imagine, or tell the "Whole Truth." As an answer to the ultimate question of Pilate's ("What is the truth?" in John 18:38), Douglas Adams's "42" from *The Hitchkiker's Guide to the Galaxy* remains as good as any other.

Contenting ourselves as best we can with what truths we do know, we tend to identify Beauty with the not-true because we find so much of our experience boring, painful, or morally repulsive. Therefore we suppose that a true description of ordinary life must not be beautiful, and that a beautiful description cannot be true. *Truth is not Beauty* we assert. The truths we know do not seem to us beautiful, and attention to Beauty can prevent us from perceiving some truths. We are normally surrounded by beauty which we tend to ignore, and to which art can draw our attention. We sympathize with St. Bernard, who is said to have taken long walks while pondering Truth during which he would from time to time strike off the heads of flowers at the side of his path. Their beauty interrupted his spiritual meditations—it was irrelevant, distracting—and, because Beauty can be distracting or irrelevant to our intentions, we reject the urn's assertion that Beauty is Truth.

Truth, we say, is a matter of survival—and thus to know or say the Truth is more important than to recognise or make Beauty. Thus we tend to believe that by rejecting Beauty we come closer to the Truth. But many truths cannot be told without Beauty. Was Matthew Brady, the American Civil War photographer, telling falsehoods when, it is rumoured, he rearranged corpses for the purpose of making more effective photographs? His beautiful (and horrifying) photographs tell us more about the war than do less skilled photographs of the same scenes. And who has told us more Truth about war than Goya? But we can't claim that Goya's etchings are not beautiful.

Consider the artless accounts of reporters, diarists, letter writers—people who go out of the way to report "just the facts" (as if dullness were always more truthful than the well-written). These do not tell us as much about the world we inhabit as can the beauty of a work of art. Art can make Truth more visible, more powerful—and more inhabitable. Art can tell us where we are in the universe, how we feel, how things happen—art explains, it demonstrates—as the cliché goes: "it brings alive."

Art, making Beauty, informs us.

Keats's urn shows us its joy face, showing Beauty as a pause in time, immortal because out of time. But an urn, a work of art, might as easily show us its pain face, showing us Beauty within time, mortal, temporary—and as overwhelmingly beautiful as the urn's joy face, but showing instead suffering, passion, madness, grief, terror. This Beauty, this Truth, may also be all we know or need to know. It does not reconcile. If we want to know the truth about what it is to be human, we need art to tell us. We need both faces of Keats's urn.

2. *The Urn's Joy Face*

Poetry that shows us the urn's "pain face" continues to be written. But to judge by awards, reviews, grants, praise, publisher's choices—serious poetry is out of fashion. Most art, and, nowadays I think, most poetry, is intended to amuse, much like Walt Disney's Mary Poppins who provides "a spoonful of sugar" to "make the medicine go down"—but without any "medicine." Of course we don't need "medicine" all the time—people "mutht be amuthed," as Dickens's Sleary (*v. Hard Times*) reminds us. The "joy face" of the urn is as valuable as the "pain face," but I have come to believe that in today's poetry and writing about poetry there is too much sugar.

Six indications of the present bias in favour of sugar:

a) During Poetry Weekend at the University of New Brunswick there have often been readers who, before presenting their poems, apologize to their audience of fellow poets because the poems they are about to read are not amusing. They apologise for writing about sadness, death, illness; they apologise for "negative" emotions. The majority of the Poetry Weekend readers, however, stick to presenting material that will not distress the audience. (No university audience is distressed by "bad" language, only by serious topics or emotional presentations).

b) One of Canada's best poets, editing an anthology of contemporary poems, wrote in her introduction that she felt such an anthology was and should be like entering a party: genial conversation, good music, great food and drink—everyone having wonderfully convivial time. Yet almost all of the major poets have written at one time or another dark, distressing poems—do we make them empty their pockets before they can come in? Granted, some poets (such as G.K. Chesterton) would be good party poets, but... Hopkins? Dickinson? Hardy? By preferring party poems as much as she could, the editor skewed the anthology. (Of course the poems submitted to her were probably selected by editors who shared her bias).

c) Recently a new literary magazine, whose name I omitted to write down, declared that it would "eschew" publishing the "overly personal." But the personal is where all poetry begins. There are, I agree, some subjects not suitable for public chatter, but poetry and prose fiction, demanding as artworks more of our private attention, should not be so confined. Should we censor the musings of Leopold Bloom? (Perhaps what the magazine meant by "overly personal" were feminist subjects like menstruation?) There are no subjects and no emotions unsuitable for poetry. There are only two kinds of poetry: poetry that seems to have been written with ink, and can be intelligent, charming, serious or cosy—but always cool—and poetry which seems to have been written in blood: passionate, personal, and sometimes uncomfortable. As Walt Whitman writes in *Leaves of Grass*, "Who touches this, touches a man."

d) At present, critics, editors, judges, and teachers of creative writing overvalue "innovative" form—not original insight, not re-examination of language use (as the first postmodernists recommended)—but innovative form, which is a mechanical skill. There are at least two aspects of the "innovative" that affect the sugar content of contemporary verse: first, the contention that verbal disarray reflects or represents the chaos or disorder of nature and the inadequacy of language to convey much "meaning." This leads to a rejection of narrative, argument, or symbolic representation, and, with its emphasis on disruption of "meaning" leads to a refusal to deal with the distressing—a cop-out I think. Second, "innovative" carries with it a rejection of the supposed formalities and emotional seriousness of the past, perhaps especially a rejection of the extremely personal, highly emotional, embarrassing poetry of the great poets who immediately preceded us. Plaths don't party. They embarrass us. (There is no prejudice against poems vehemently expressing opinions and attitudes the audience already has, and is comfortable with possessing).

e) Even the least "innovative" of our poets are affected by our desire to be amused and pleased. Our nature-loving poets nearly all produce poems describing the natural beauty of forests, fields, beaches, backyards as being unsullied, un-endangered places where one can serenely meditate Beauty (or at least prettiness). The most popular poets, such as Mary Oliver, produce poems as accessible and as sugary as the paintings of Norman Rockwell. The best Canadian poetry, we are led to suppose, has a "positive" attitude—rather like the Monty Python song, sung by Brian while being crucified (*v. Life of Brian*): "Always Look on the Bright Side."

f) The peddling of literary artifacts as amusements, or "play," seems to me a sign of the current degeneration of postmodernism from its original emphasis on thoughtful inquiry to a mere display of disconnection. A major Canadian publisher is currently promoting a sequence of titbit texts by Molly Peacock as "delish"—like tiny chocolates. This material, a not uncharming variation on the parlour game "I Love My Love With an A Because Her Name is Amanda," does without the narrative force or semantic interest of, say, "The Young Lady From Twickenham," and is accompanied by pictures that rarely refer to the text nor suggest possible alternate narrative. Pure innovation. Purely postmodernist. Sugar.

There is no harm and indeed much pleasure in sugar now and then. But if this is what we mostly ingest, we will die of spiritual malnutrition. We need to value the "pain face" of the urn. Pleasure without pain is not Truth—and playfulness is not Beauty. Yet there is still much beautiful pain poetry being written which we should value more than we apparently do."

John Nyman

Slogan, Substance, Dream

Like all manifestos, my manifesto is in debt. It is indebted to many poetries and people, but not because it has gained much from them; my manifesto is in the red. Behind it are politically bankrupt formalisms, intellectually bankrupt lyricisms, and morally bankrupt avant-gardisms. Fortunately, there is no bankruptcy in language; there is always another poetry. But the poetry that credits my manifesto is yet to come.

Immersed in neoliberal capitalism, my manifesto seeks to shore up this poetry by speculating on language. Caliban says, "You taught me language; and my profit on't / Is, I know how to curse." My manifesto is in that hole. Like all manifestos, it pictures itself climbing out of Hell.

Slogan

In January of 2017, a poem called "I Woke Up" appeared in *Poetry*. The poem reads, "and it was political. / I made coffee and the coffee was political. / I took a shower and the water was." Later it reads, "That I didn't know how to grieve when another person was killed in America / was political, and it was political when America killed another person, / who they were and what color and gender and who I am in relation." And finally, "I thought I was not a political poet and still / my imagination was political. / It had been, this whole time I was asleep." The poem was written by Jameson Fitzpatrick.

Often we say "the personal is political." No one claims ownership of this phrase, but many are invested in it. And many aren't. Does this make it more or less true? I call "the personal is political" a slogan because it doesn't matter that it's true; what matters is that I'm invested in it.

A slogan doesn't say what is or what should be or what should be done. A slogan is a way of doing by saying, and by saying something it becomes something. A slogan makes itself said. Ditto for poetry. I'm invested in poetry because poetry shows up, whether or not it shows me the or a world, myself, or anything else. It's not about waking up. Jameson Fitzpatrick takes for granted that the personal is political. But to say "the personal is political" is to take nothing for granted; it means investing in what you say, creating the concerns you speak of, and making them matter. What is Jameson Fitzpatrick invested in? Personally, I can't help reading "I Woke Up" as a kind of satire—of being "woke," or of "waking up" to the truth that the personal is political without investing in anything. Or, at least, without investing in anything different than what you were invested in asleep.

I'm invested in the content of poetry—that is, its body, what it incorporates. Anything counts as content if I invest in it. For example, a poetry's form can be its content. But a responsible poetry strives to become constituted. It lives its own skin. A responsible poetry doesn't cower from embodiment (the body of its texts, the bodies of its audience). It doesn't seek life in the bodies of others.

Poetry is not a public service. Poetry is about making a public: the readership, thinkership, and writership that amasses at its topic (its *topos*, the place of *this* poetry).

Substance

I'm invested in an open poetry, but not a poetry that attracts all investors equally. My poetry is open like a book, not like a bank. I'm invested in a vulnerable poetry, in a poetry that makes itself vulnerable whether its position is strong or weak. My poetry is a particular thing.

I'm invested in a poetry that shows its substance, that *is* its substance. But what's substance?

> It's like a signature, but it doesn't belong to its author. (It's not an intellectual property.)

> It's like experience, but it can't be distributed arbitrarily. (It's not a kind of capital.)

> ~~To Hell with the poetry of possession, of financial, social, cultural, and intellectual capital.~~

It's like identity (like blood), but it isn't transferred determinately from producer to product (from father to son).

John Nyman

It's like belief, but it doesn't guarantee solidarity with others composed of the same substance.

~~To Hell with the poetry of the self, which acts as if the self were already poetry.~~

It's like flavour, but it touches more than taste.

It's like style, but it isn't clothing. (It's not the opposite of nudity.)

~~To Hell with the poetry of consumption, swallowed and shit out.~~

It's more than what it substantiates, but less than infinitely variable. My poetry pulls you in a direction.

It's like content, but it isn't contained.

~~To Hell with metaphysical poetry, with true and abstract poetry, with poetry thinner than air.~~

Substance finds no alibi in the innocence of process; when it shows up, it shows up complete.

You can apologize for it, but it's still responsible for being exactly what it is.

~~To Hell with the poetry of paratext, with didactic illegible poetry, with the ever-unfinished experiment.~~

It's like a dream everyone catches you dreaming. Its shame is yours to shoulder, its glory yours to grandstand.

~~To Hell with provocateur poetry, with aversive poetry, with the poetry of "it's only poetry."~~

I'm invested in a poetry with substance.

John Nyman

Dream

> *I recognize that life is a dream, and I dream lucid*
> —J. Cole, "Fire Squad"

I'm dreaming as I write this, but I'm not asleep. My dreams don't just happen to me; they belong to me. My dreams are mine—open and vulnerable. What happens to me is reality, because I'm awake. But I'm invested in a poetry that dreams.

Dreams aren't a puzzle, a symptom, or an artifact. They aren't unconscious. Dreams are the ideals I act with and the wishes I work on. I make them like I make a gesture, have them like a haircut. Dreams don't hold a hidden meaning; they are what they mean.

We're all awake, and we're all dreaming. But we don't all have the same dreams. A dream belongs to whoever dreams it, to whoever invests in it, and it belongs to reality as much as its dreamers do. I'm invested in a poetry that belongs to reality.

I'm invested in an idealism (of art, of poetry) without elitism. That is to say, without any metaphor of verticality. To write poetry is to occupy a tiny niche of human existence, no more the pinnacle of that existence than its lowest depth. The poetry I'm invested in is idealistic, but it recognizes that there's nothing special about a good idea.

Vanguard or rear guard, the poetry I'm invested in looks forward from where it already stands. It doesn't have to choose between a shared reality and its own ideals. And though it takes incredible responsibility to hold to both of these positions at once, the poets I'm invested in are really no one unusual. They write with their feet on the ground and their heads floating in the sky.

Dani Spinosa

Visual Poetry for Women

This is not a manifesto urging us to remedy the persistent gender gap in visual poetics. I've done that work already. And other, more thorough historians have done that work better. Alex Balgiu and Mónica de la Torre's *Women in Concrete Poetry 1959–1979* is illuminating for the gaps it reveals even in my knowledge. Other writers like Amanda Earl and Jessica Smith have done brilliant work collecting and highlighting more recent work by women and gender non-conforming poets and language artists. That work is important. It serves to remedy several decades of neglect. But I arrive here with a hunger for overwriting, a desire to stop revision, and present instead this voice louder than the story that's already been told, that's still telling. I want to carve several new names into the concrete.

Welcome, ladies. Now we're writing like we own the place.

Take it Into Your Own Hands

If women are to achieve that longed for 1:1 ratio for appearances in anthologies, journals, reviews, and other gatekeeper methods of canon-establishment and movement solidifying, they must refuse to define their visual poetics against the poetics that has been heretofore written and published and historicized by men. The best way to do this, of course, is to seize the means of literary production. Seize. Quite literally, take it into your hands. In the past, this seizing has meant for me the work of the analogue (hand-stitching, screen print, and once painstakingly and uncomfortably removing the wings of a dead cicada I found on my porch for Kate Siklosi). I have come to embrace the seizing of the means of digital production here, too, particularly for the ways that it allows us to take old media into our own hands. It strikes me as strange, how few stories you hear of secretaries bludgeoning their bosses mid-dictation. Take it into your own hands, girl. Make the ratio you want to see in the world.

Don't Resist Signification

Part of what they've done—what we've all done—is make visual poetics a place where signifiers go to die, get slipped slipshod from their signifieds. What if a hallmark of feminist visual poetry is the reintroduction of the process of signification into the visual poem, the appearance of that smooth-talking lyrical

Dani Spinosa

subject where she's not supposed to be? I'm not saying you should believe her. You should not believe her. She is, necessarily, a liar. But I'm saying, let her in. I'm here to tell you that words are okay, they're all right. They are not dooming you to some kind of lyrical wasteland. It serves no one to assume the asemic or the nonsensical is superior to sense. They need each other. Let yourself write a word. Let yourself write a sentence. I write visual poetry with a lyric I. She's dotted with a heart. I write a lyric I that writing workshops and poetry professors told me to suppress very early on. Find the voice they told you to quiet down and make it louder.

We Are Living in the Digital World

I am writing in early 2021 and I do not have you tell you that our world is deeply embedded in the digital. Today I do so much online: banking, teaching, planning events with friends. Not to mention the meeting I'm currently attending while I write this, camera off, on mute. Where has my body gone in these days? What has happened to my hands? The digital, as scholars have so often told me, is named after my fingers and toes. It both touches me all the time and leaves my name floating aimlessly in cyberspace. It is in the air, and it's a series of tubes. Don't mistake one for the other.

And I am a Digital Girl

The mistake I mean is two mistakes. The first is to say that we have become digital beings, and so the digital has become the place where we make art, the ideal space of the poetic. This is the mistake that says: why do with my hands what I can get my computer to do for free? This is the mistake of a techno-utopianism and I am guilty of it often. The visual poet has affordances with the emergence of personal and networked computing that our predecessors could barely dream of. Every time I use a clone stamp or an eraser or copy and paste a letter, I feel slightly guilty for standing on the shoulders of my analogue predecessors and cheating so. The second and arguably worse mistake is to say that we have become digital beings, and so I will take my art as far outside of the digital as I can, to idealize an outside. The visual poet today owes it to her fingers to get them into as many spaces as possible. Touch screens and keys and thread and ink and paper and pen and other fingers. The digital is a network. Use it to touch.

Dani Spinosa

All the Power's in the Mess

In Kate Boyer's and Kim England's exceptional study of the gendering of work and its relation to technology, they recognize that the feminization of clerical work and the automation of office work by way of the electric typewriter and the dictaphone were co-constitutive. They argue that "[a]s a new occupation in the late nineteenth century, typing was gender-neutral." But by the middle of the century, the advertisements focused on portability as well as the use of the typewriter in the home, and thus implied that clerical work might be "the 'proper' place for middle-class women." At first, the typewriter was implemented to be nice and clean. It standardized and made uniform all the various idiosyncrasies of handwriting. Typing's feminization cleaned up not just women's writing, but the female presence in the workplace. It allowed women to engage in such masculine activities as being in an office, writing, and earning an income without sacrificing a chaste, bourgeois femininity. So, any feminist visual poetry using the typewriter *should* be messy on some level in order to counteract the neoliberalist professional desire to ensure women's voices—and actions, and bodies, and bodies, and bodies—fit tidily into their designated boxes, coded feminine.

Coded Feminine

And yet, that feminized typewriter has been for a long time the tool of all writing, including visual poetry for men. It was designed for serious work and it produced serious work. For every officeful of secretaries taking dictation, there was a Kerouac with his thick roll of paper, a McCaffery with all his papers lining up perfectly. But, do not worry. Plenty of other things in your home, beyond your typewriter, have been gendered feminine in order to maintain a chaste cleanliness of the domestic body.

Coded Poetry

These things are, but are not limited to: threads, fabrics, hooks, yarns, plants, herbs, flowers, paints, waxes, powders and creams, craft supplies, especially children's craft supplies, magazines, hosiery, and jewelry. These items coded feminine are now, as we digital bodies embrace a merger with the analogue, becoming major features in visual and mixed media poetics by writers coded feminine across the world. There are many femme language artists using these analogue and feminized

Dani Spinosa

items to produce beautiful work right now. Yesterday I was thinking all day of Jessica Bebenek translating *The Waste Land* into a knitting pattern. Today I am wondering about Hiromi Suzuki translating magazines into collages into GIFs. It feels like once a day for the last year I've thought of Astra Papachristodoulou suspending poems in resin. Now is a good time to be a femme making a beautiful mess.

Insist on Your Own History

I feel like I waited a long time for people to write the books I wanted to read. I waited longer for people to write the histories of visual poetry that would include women. I got tired of waiting. So did Amanda Earl, and the forthcoming publication of *Judith* through Timglaset is the result of that. This is also necessarily a call to make your own stuff. Get to know the people at your local print shop. Pirate some software. Become a small press. Don't wait until you sound more like a poet; you already sound like a poet. Don't wait until you have more connections; the only real connection you need is your fingers touching paper or keys or both. Write your own history. Insist on your own bias.

Remove the Phallocentricity

When we make our own books and write our own histories it is no longer an effort to fill an existing gap, to remedy a lack. I am not interested in supplementing or supplanting. I'm advocating instead for a utopian writing practice where women in visual poetics might write as if the histories of visual poetics we've always been told were histories where women were the ones doing the typing. I want to envision my mothers language—and her mother's, and my father's mother's, and their mothers'—as a visual poetics. I have—we have—spent enough time demonstrating my abilities, meeting the minimum criteria, answering the pop quiz of have you read him or him or him. I'm writing now as if a history of phallocentricity hasn't been the dominant history of visual poetics. And I'm reminded every day that it is not. It need not be. It hasn't been. It's gone.

Dare to Be Not Very Good

If there was one lesson I could impart on my younger selves, on young women writing poetry, and especially young women interested in visual poetry, it would

Dani Spinosa

be to let yourself make—and share—bad poetry. I have often said, following some very funny friends of mine, that visual poets are people who aren't very good poets and also aren't very good artists. I don't mean this as an insult. I mean that visual poetics has the capacity to render both poetry and visual art down to their constituent parts, and to thus work a bit—slowly—at stripping away the elitism and vanguardism and access barriers that go alongside something called talent. If you allow yourself to make "bad" things, you allow yourself to experiment and grow. Visual poetics turns letters into shapes, turns meaning into one small part of the poem. Let that free you to make something weird, shitty, and transformative.

Sound Stupid

Alongside your bad poetry, you should let yourself sound stupid. I mean this, too, in a good way. Let your shoulders relax into your lilting ditzy cadences. Release your "likes" and "uhms" like starlings all fluttering and invasive. Say smart things with elongated vocal fry. There is no reason that visual poetics needs to be the site of intellectualism as a sign of status. The whole point is to disrupt those semantic structures that we need to sound like intellectuals. Say big, philosophical, theoretical things in your own voice, girl. That "like" is the best place for this disruption. It's what those fancy French philosophers were talking about. Trust.

All Design is Political

Remember, too, even as you make your bad poems, draw your bad pictures, share your bad work, that every design choice you make is a political one. In this plague year I have learned a lot from the artist, designer, and poet Kevin Yuen Kit Lo who writes of the political act of design and its power to work against or disrupt white supremacy. I believe, too, that the design choices we make in feminist visual poetics might work to disrupt, in small, meaningful ways, the phallo- and phallogo-centricity of this industry. I believe the design choices of the vast and varied array of femmes that have tread this ground before us have begun that work. I hope to leave small, meaningful spaces for the femmes who will come after me.

Dani Spinosa

Writing is Séance

And so we must not forget as we innovate that all writing is a summoning of ghosts. Visual poetics may not be so concerned with the meaning of the incantations, but we know what we write as femmes in this industry is not a palimpsest—oh, how the academic has overwritten and overridden this term—but a spell repeated and repeated, a ghost that keeps visiting. Hello.

Refuse Dictation, Define Yourself in the Positive

I recommend refusing dictation, babes. Not that you accepting it before, but … we all were, a little, doing that, some of the time. Write the books men backchannel to tell you it's not what they wanted you to write. Speak the way that makes people surprised you're so brilliant. Make one or several bad mistakes in the process. Either treat every poem like an infant, or else eat your young, or else tie your tubes with typewriter ribbon and insist that the ink that drips from you is enough to finish that manuscript. I recommend counting to ten before you storm out of the office. I recommend a short manicure for the typewriter where possible; slightly longer for a touch screen is manageable; the computer keyboard will let you go long, almond, coffin, stiletto. Be prepared, though, because the noise is loud. It counts out a beat for you.

You're incanting the spell now, and it's reverberating, it's calling out femmes from their houses like children in *Hocus* fucking *Pocus*. I recommend watching five or six movies to get you through. I recommend righteous indignation until it's too exhausting, because we know it is exhausting, and when you're exhausted, I recommend focusing again and again on the beat. There's time and there's room and it's been quiet enough for long enough. But now there's like a bagillion of us and we're making quite the ruckus and I'm pretty sure people are listening and some of 'em are buying books.

Yusra Usmani

Poetry as Spectacle

1.

In the *Ets ha-Da'at*, or *Tree of Knowledge*, one finds more than a hundred spells, some including the well known incantation "abracadabra." Various theories on the phrase's origin exist: most likely from the Aramaic *avra ke-davra*, "I create as I speak."

The Sefer Yetzirah, a similarly obscure text, espouses the whole of creation, both the macrocosm of the universe and the microcosm of man, to be built upon 10 numbers and 22 letters for a total of 32 characters. The Muslim Hurufists likewise dedicated themselves to the interpretation of letters as not only phonetic markers, but as having a symbolic meaning which overrides the actual words they spell out. The Hurufuists correlated the 32 letters of the Perso-Arabic alphabet to the features of the human form. Evidence of the significance of the number 32 is seen in there being 32 teeth in the average mouth—the mouth, of course, being the instrument of language.

Across nearly every geographical region, one finds an inseparable intimacy between language and creation. Because of the natural fact of revelation being delivered through language, it is no surprise that the power inherent to language became an early subject of curiousity.

2.

While trudging through the arid desert, the prophet Muhammad and his companions met a poet, who, after reciting, faced the following reproach: "It is better for the belly of any one of you to be stuffed with pus rather than to stuff [one's mind] with poetry." In dishonest hands this record has been used in a paltry attempt to argue the sterility of an Islamically-permissible life, but the denouncement was neither an injustice nor a surprise to the early Muslims who flanked Muhammad's side.

To the pre-Islamic Arabs, various exercises of mediation between worlds were known, and it was well established to be the domain of the *jinn*, or genie. Among them is divination, or *Kihanah*, where the seer is believed to have consulted with the jinn, and the jinn's swift and non-physical nature allowed them to take news from the heavens to be delivered promptly in the heart of the seer.

Despite being theoretically metaphysical, jinns tend to have been mythologized in ways that suppose them to have physical bodies. One allegation of the jinn's methods imagined them as climbing on top of one another's shoulders until the last reached heaven. The topmost jinn overheard the gods speaking and whispered it to the one below, and the rest did the same until the message reached the jinn closest to Earth, and this jinn then told the seer. Because of the likelihood of error in oral transmission, the seer's words, although undeniably of divine origin, were considered somewhat dubious. The role of the seer overlapped with the poet, as the seer delivered findings in attractive and sophisticated prose, and also the poet, like the seer, belonged to the trade of jinn intercession.

The Kitab al-Aghani, an encyclopedic collection of Islamic literary works, abounds with anecdotes of poets and their jinn inspirers. The love poet Kuthayyir 'Azza is here recorded as saying he didn't start reciting poetry until it was first recited to him. He elaborates that he had been treading the desert near Madinah when a bizarre man on horseback commanded him to recite poetry, which he himself then began reciting. The bewildered poet asked who he was, and received the following answer: "I am your double from the jinn."

William Butler Yeats, in the 1915 poem "Ego Dominius Tuus" describes an "other" of himself, much like 'Azza's.

Another anecdote comes from Abu Amir Shuhayd, who prefaced his treatise on spirits and demons with a story composed following the loss of his beloved. Wanting to write an elegy in her dedication but overcome with grief, he was approached by a jinn who then assisted in composing the work. Shuhayd claims to have been taken on a sojourn to meet various other jinns who have inspired great poets of the past.

A verse from Hassan ibn Thabit, a poet from the time of Muhammad, reads, "Sometimes, it is he who recites poetry. Sometimes it is I."

According to one encounter, a jinn named Abu Hadrash proclaims "We are folk of clairvoyance and cleverness. We know all human beings' languages and beyond, and we have a language that men do not know." The jinn would sometimes require something in exchange for his inspiration, not too unlike the wretched pet at Faustus's side, or the modern myth of a musician selling his soul.

Poets' associations with jinns were well known to the Arabs, and this is documented in the Quran itself, which records the Meccans accusing Muhammad of being a mere poet. They are supposed to have said: "What, shall we forsake our gods for a poet possessed?"

Islamic cosmology conceptualizes three realms: the terrestrial, the imaginal, and the celestial, which are not entirely independent of each other, but subject to constant exchange. The imaginal or intermediate realm is ascribed to the jinn. Ibn Arabi, the great Islamic philospher, describes the realm itself as being "like the line that separates the sun and its shadow." In the imaginal, forms shift and interact in an unusual way, much like anyone who's immersed themselves in the throes of frenzied inspiration knows—it moves in wild directions, bound to different laws. The happenings in this realm are like dreams which collapse into one another. They are not entirely illogical, but only abide to an internal logic.

Popular Islam is generally suspicious of the frenzied state of the inbetween. For example, the prophet Muhammad forebade sitting between the shade and sun and advised against going outside at precarious times of day, warning his companions that "the devils come out when the sun sets, until the first part of the night is over." His disavowal of poetry is therefore not only due to it being a shady source of revelation, but also its cosmological nature. However, what Islam has suggested about poetry, from both the Quran and the traditions of Muhammad, only disparages poets without contradicting the assumptions already made of them in Arab culture.

In Greek tradition, the poet is a mere mouthpiece for the muses—a much less cunning figure than the jinn, but an all the same supernatural occurrence. As Homer begins the *Odyssey* with the invocation "Sing in me, Muse, and through me tell the story of that man skilled in all ways of contending," he makes explicit his status as a mere instrument. Socrates, in *Ion*, speaks of a poet named Tynnichus of Chalcis, who apparently wrote nothing of any significance until the intervention of the gods, and Socrates concludes "it is not they who utter these precious revelations while their mind is not within them, but it is the god himself who speaks, and through them becomes articulate to us." The correlation between the soothsayers and poets made obvious in pre-Islamic Arabian culture is also corroborated by Socrates, for the poets, according to him, "are like diviners or soothsayers who also say many fine things, but do not understand the meaning of them." Divination had its public representatives such as the Pythia of Delphi, who, according to historians, wrote in an incomprehensible manner. The client would have to take the written piece to a professional interpreter. This incomprehnsiblity is mimicked in the Christian conception of speaking in tongues, for the man who speaks tongues is entirely unintelligible as he utters the mysteries of the spirit.

The Spanish concept of El-Duende is both a spirit which enters the body and the emotion itself—an artistic ecstasy, an irrationality, and a heightened sensitivity. The artist mustn't give in entirely, but engage in a skillful battle as the duende grasps both the artist and audience. According to the flamenco singer Manuel Torre, it is a "mysterious power which everyone senses and no philosopher explains." Its realms are most often music, dance, and spoken poetry.

In a letter to an acquaintance, the great Romantic poet John Keats says "I remember you saying that you had notions of a good genius presiding over you—I have of late had the same thought," and though he makes no reference to whether it be by the name of jinn, muse or duende, the sensation of having the influence of some seraphic, absurd "other" has been expressed, and further suggests the universality of the poetic spirit.

Though the origin of every poet's voice varies, it is not the poets themselves speaking, but something else that is speaking through them. One of the most obvious heirs of this conception is the prodigious and somewhat mythic Arthur Rimbaud. In 1870, after returning from his first flight to the Parisian literary scene, the sixteen-year-old Rimbaud settled again into his hometown where he met Charles Bretagne—a highly unusual gentleman who schooled him in various ancient occult philosophies, magic, and Cabbala. From then on, poetry was no longer an expression of Rimbaud's self, nor the inescapable squalor which surrounded him—for poetry, and vice itself, was now a method of reaching beyond. Rimbaud's poetry thereby transitioned from obscene and scatological outrage-pieces to the symbolist works that solidified his reputation. In a declarative letter to his old friend Georges Izambard, Rimbaud puts the position of the poet succinctly: "I is another."

3.

The word ecstasy comes from Greek *ekstasis*, "to stand outside of or transcend." The ecstatic worshipper throughout history has meditated, danced, or otherwise bewildered his mind to achieve this end and thereby unite with a higher power, which is the principal aim of mystic religion. The trance is generally triggered by a ritualistic beginning such as a brief hymn, the sounding of percussion instruments, a change in rate of drumming, the fragrance of an incense, or the act of kneeling. It is not the stimuli itself that triggers the ecstatic trance, but expectation that the stimuli marks. Therefore, this expectation is an invitation which can be anything, even, say, the opening of a book of poems.

Dionysus, god of oppositions, is also much linked with ecstasy. Dionysian ritual is both associated with wild uproar and deathlike silence; the women who followed him danced wildly as often as they stood still, staring into the abyss. He is both sensuality and cruelty, at once the fullness of life, which, in its ultimate exuberance, reaches a seething violence unto death. He embodies differences which are so stark in their extremity that they become the same thing. Oppositions send worshippers' minds reeling upon contemplation, and forces them to enter a state inaccessible to intelligence. Only the soul gains admittance.

One finds a similar principle in the Old Testament's God who is both Alpha and Omega. Especially to a Mormon, "feeling the spirit" is an integral part of faith and much of that practice is elicited by the spectacle of Christian worship. A trance may be brought on by being possessed by the mysteries of the spirit, like the man at the podium preaching the word invested in him.

4.

The benefit poetry possesses is twofold. A poet disregards himself for the spirit invested in him. A reader gives in to the work without involving himself.

As termed by John Keats, a reader employs his "negative capability," an ability to "accept uncertainties, mysteries, and doubts, without any irritable reaching after fact and reason." My goal in comparing philosophies of various traditions is not to inquire about the historic relationship between them, but to sift away their idiosyncrasies and suggest the teachings of some Universal Person:

Yusra Usmani

"A person needs something outside of their comprehension to revere, or else they make an idol out of their own intelligence. For example, the multivalent absurdities of a god who's both the first and last, the manifest and hidden, the creator and destroyer—mystery is necessary to preserve humility. The excess of religious art and architecture thrills the mind, excites the senses, and overwhelms the logical faculties. This way, providence can touch the spirit, which is taken immediately and entirely. If poetry is for the same ends, the same means are required: it should be spectacular, meaning an inherently complicated drama is reduced to its associated sounds, symbols, and sensations, which then take on a life of their own. The mind is thus filled with a lurid and disorienting perfume, and with its guard down, the spirit is captured."

5.

To use poetry as a religious instrument, the poet must tread carefully. First, the spirit of inspiration approaches the poet in search of its own self-expression. The poet has been tasked with giving it physical form. In gaining physical form, the spirit speaks through the individual elements of a literary work. The poet expands and molds these into a comprehensive piece. Although the spirit is always somewhat stifled in the world of tangible things, it is possible to uncover and directly hear its voice. To do this, the poet will reduce each element to what is precisely attached to the spirit.

As a poet edits they merely ensure each of the abstractions harmonise with one another. Like an archaeologist mending a foreign artefact, their beliefs, ideals, desire, logic, and pride are put aside in service of something beyond them. When the work is complete, even they don't know what it is. Eventually someone with the task of decipherment may come along and procure each symbol's meaning, but antecedent to that task is to first obtain the relic. This, principally, is the poet's work.

Robert Colman

Perfectly Imperfect

Do you live to work, or work to live? A question I was asked endlessly in the first ten years after I graduated from McGill, before the meme-ification and inspiration-porn acceleration of this cliché by social media. Eventually, this question led to another question: *What does work mean to me?* When I began to write poetry, the nature of labour became a central aesthetic and philosophic concern, and offshoots of this enquiry drove my artisitic practice. Since that time, I've been driven to examine my connection to labour and that of others, and poetry has seemed the ideal medium.

*

In a carpenter's workshop a few years ago, I witnessed a pristine dining room table beaten with chains by a carpenter to provide his customer with the battered, "handmade" look they wished for, as if the table had survived a long journey on a sea-tossed galleon.

*

Working in my home office on a late spring day, the window open, I listen to classic rock music along with the team working on renovations half a block away. In the stillness of the afternoon, it seemed to be just us, all moving at a desultory pace, slow enough that I noticed each time a power tool was picked up, another screw anchored into wood, the bit grinding as its purchase reached its limit. That fricative *ck-ck-ck* was a reminder of why work poetry, particularly work poetry focused on manual tasks, is so appealing to write, and often to hear. A landscape of sound and touch, ready-made. A hammer provides the bluntest percussion behind each process. A manual screwdriver provides the quiet rending of softer woods, a sibilance, but in its final realization, the bite and grip of connection. A handsaw repeats its endless trochee. Power tools can choke complaint or spin a fast violin, depending on the task. Likewise, a lathe or mill will signal beauty or a bastard chunk of rot in their tone. Further: the hiss of gas as a welder sparks an arc, the stacked dimes we see in the perfectly realized weld seam. There is an auditory and visual feast in reaching for the completion of an act. And I've only spoken of the tools, leaving aside the sweat, the muscle groups in hand, arm, back and core asking to be recognized, moving from the twist of the screw, the

Robert Colman

pressure on the angle grinder. These acts also engage the ear of the listener. As we watch and hear the music of work, the person engaged in creating this music is also watching and listening, coordinating the muscle memory with auditory and visual input, all of this their instrument and solo or symphony, depending on the work being done—completion of a single assembly or the erection of a structure. Stanzas. Rooms.

*

Work is perhaps the most graspable tool we have to metaphorize the strive for perfection, or at least realisation. I invoke here Max Weber's conception of the Protestant work ethic as the basis of modern capitalism, and how the spirit of capitalism reflects a set of values, namely hard work and progress. In Weber's sense, one that manifested in my childhood, we are machines of labour, performing the "good work" of honest toil. The machines we use are extensions of our own desire for good or completion, and are therefore a natural place to examine ourselves. For me, scenes of work are a more instinctive place to reach for metaphor than nature. As a "citified" poet, I've a tenuous reach for natural detail, the necessary panoply of flora and fauna understood in every season as a landscape rather than isolated object. I do not see the trees for the forest, but I do see each worker, each part they are playing in making and remaking our world.

*

Though machines work toward a goal, are we in sync with that goal? Or are we subsumed by it? The noise of work interrupts and cajoles thought, and the poem fights through toward its own conclusion.

*

Paradoxically, the appeal for writers and readers of literary works is that perfection and completion aren't guaranteed. Like the structure of a poem, the design of a part or an object has its own particular rules and expectations. Because we are human and part of the natural world, we are imperfect. We are told that work will bring us closer to perfection, but in the push and pull of faith, we begin to respect the nature of failure. We rebel against the perfection that is unrealizable in ourselves, that is not in our nature. Yet we seem to make machines that are perfect, machines that work to make our created world more ergonomic. We are accustomed to flawlessly machined objects that are mass-produced every day. So it is that we have a casual relationship with perfection. The parallel with a great poem is obvious: some literary works approach perfection, the pinnacle of beauty, and our relationship with them is often casual, too.

*

Failure is a part of art. Consider *Kintsugi*, the Japanese art of repairing broken pottery with lacquer dust or precious metals. The damage is the beauty, the lived reality. Travelling in Japan some years ago, researching a number of potteries, I struggled to find what, to me, would be the perfect sake set. Everything was too precise. Eventually, I found a cup that looked like it was made of petrified beach sand and a carafe in a muddy lustre, indentations where nature would ask a finger and thumb to cradle it. It was, and remains, perfect to me for the tactility suggested in its roughness. In the work poem, the question is, what is on the edge of breaking? The machine? The individual? The connection between the two?

*

As part of my day job, I visit factories and interview owners and operators in an attempt to tell their stories. Occasionally even I hear what it means for a machine to fail. A spindle judders, a weld gun burns through a seam. Older tradespeople bemoan the lack of skilled younger people to take their place in the workforce, but even those there to replace them don't yet have the visual and auditory database of years on the job squirrelled away in their heads to know, for instance, when an automated mill isn't running at peak efficiency. They may not know from listening that a welding gun is in disrepair, or that gas isn't being delivered to the arc in precisely the right way. It's no different, in some measures, to listening for the right word to find its way into a poem. The muscle memory that tells you when a line hisses against another, yelling to be uncoupled. And as a poet, I want to extend a hand across that same divide, capture what is both perfect and imperfect in the act of making.

Robert Colman

*

The ideal contemporary work poem strikes me as one that says "this exists"; not a tool of education as such, but a poetry of the individual dialects that distinguish one workplace from another. For example, welders are somewhat famous for having their own language on job sites. It's a communal understanding built on having a varied but specific skill. Being able to peek behind the curtains of this world has a unique appeal and power.

*

Most machinists get experience with manual lathes and mills in their early training, but they move on to automated technology quickly because that's what's necessary to be productive in the modern world. The sense of "feel" they develop, then, is rudimentary, at best. Physical connection gets abstracted. Machinists are not alone. Their senses slowly unlatch from the physicality of making, not unlike me typing this paragraph at a rapid pace, with my snaking fingers on a slim laptop. The deliberation in the use of a manual typewriter would slow me, would change the process of how my thoughts are formed. I don't want to be beholden to the past, but the poem itself wants that *clack*, the Olympian typist's strong fingers, the deft flight of the hard return. A tool that wants to be gripped. Every one of our senses are affected by these distances. The work poem spans that gap, celebrates connection's diminuendo.

*

A Canadian company recently unveiled a sensor that will record an automated welding setup and let you know if, from the sound, it may be out of spec. The poem wants to tell it better. Someone has to react to the sensors. We're still in a place where signals need translation into human action. But what happens when that's no longer the case? What happens when a bot can perfectly interpret an issue in a weld and automatically adjust the automated welder? What happens when every cut and bend, every turned part and milled piece can be achieved without hands? Is this the future of AI – perfectly capturing an interview, efficiently interpreting a discussion? Even now, I visit fewer factories, depending on reported description to piece together place. Where is the smell of oil? The sweet toxicity of the weld plume? Is our good work now this cleanliness? How do we redefine our connection with it in tandem?

*

The language of an office job may be less broad in its linguistic opportunities, but only because it has already achieved a level of automation previously unachievable in other workplaces. How often do I use paper now compared to 20 years ago? How rare is a fax machine? A telephone call? What slight noise do I make on this keyboard? There is no ink to slam thickly on foolscap.

There is still purpose, though. Still a want in this doing, if not quite joy in doing it. We need to know, and find the ideal language with which to approach that knowing.

*

Upon reflection, I realize that many of my own work-related poems were attempts at wresting power from an office dynamic that seemed to be crushing me and those around me. In capturing the absurdities of panic created by an imploding work environment – layoffs, dwindling sales, low morale – I was creating a reasoned perspective, a way in which to step out of that situation and remove some of its control. Escaping its clutch, I clutched it in turn. I could fathom not needing it, if only abstractly, for brief slivers of time. Work ethic had betrayed me, and the poems wished to explain how. But in opposition, Weber's insight was still my anchor.

*

Tom Wayman believes that a literature "that does not regard and depict work as central to the human story is immature." Any literature that ignores work certainly avoids tackling a point of conflict for every individual. What is the engine in this relationship? What drives, and what is driven? Poetry allows a dissection and reimagining of the parts, the impetus. Roles reverse and morph every day and we adapt. I adapt. I say I adapt, but it is adapting to this question for which I have no answer: What of work do we know? No answer but in the non-answers written out as poems.

White Pine

James Lindsay

How Does It Feel

There's a filter on the window,
meant to protect us from the harsh

afternoon sunlight. But all it seems
to do is make the room unnecessarily

blue as you merge with the furniture,
the white lamp and aqua sofa, in ways

the Swedes never intended. Trapped
behind the vista veil, handless sleeves

flap like a drowning things' flippers.
I don't understand your massive sweater.

You swim in its cobalt while the cold glow
of the lightbox and its rotating ski scene

illuminates your contemplative face.
You chew a pen but take no notes on

that murky inbetweenness, the timbre
of dreams fading as blonde hair turtles

into a high woolen neckline as you
emerge from under plush bedding

that belongs to a hotel room you paid for,
therefore, entitled to explore as you see fit.

So make an aqueduct of your body to bridge
the chairs and when you find the costume

jewelry, concealed within a hardcover,
pause for a minute to pose with it, breathing.

James Lindsay

Double Self-Portrait

*I wanted to make a picture coming out
of a literary source in the idea*

*of the double in which the identity
of the character was maybe not*

concludable, so I tucked my grey
sweatshirt into my belted blue

jeans to better match my lookalike.
He wore wine-dark corduroys

that compliment our couch. "Red,"
I said when I first saw it. "It's red."

"More mauve than cherry," said
my blushing double, arms crossed

and hesitant to invite you to sit in
the white wire chair you referred to

as a flipped arachnid dead in its web,
backlit by heatstroke and twin domestic.

It's safe to assume that one of us sired
the other, grafted himself to the sofa

corner where a pink blanket peeled
back; cracked the door and took a nap

in practical cibachrome Vancouver,
awakening later that afternoon

as brother-fathers to one another,
both in incest and attendance.

Virginia Konchan

Name me transient

Name me transient, name me obligatory.
Name me hindsight, name me plenty.
The theme of this place is savagery.
The river's mouth needs something.
It's a drama. An interrogative sentence
wells up inside me. Have you grown
accustomed to a lifestyle
no one can provide?
She had no need of fox furs.
She had ceased to exist.
No one ever asks whether flowers
should be permanent.
I should be permanent.
Name me lost wages.
What does it feel like
to have a voice that carries
without making a sound?
Count your fingers.
Count your calluses.
Count the miles to the state line.
I will sign my name in Cyrillic.
I will shut my eyes like a sad man.
Name me modesty, name me vexation.
They said it would hurt, and it does.
This is the black, shot with blue.
Count yourself among the counted.
That spark reminds me of you.

Virginia Konchan

Here is your face

Here is your face, your face:
unshakable hallelujah.
That's as real and vital to me now
as my gnarled hand
holding up a morning glory
in your boyhood garden.
What is desire but the hardwire
argument given to the mind's
unstoppable mouth?
My feet have fumbled for you, following
like secret service men, a clue, a song.
Your trace eludes me;
your near-kiss was the truce.
Often I am permitted to return to a meadow
as if it were a given property of the mind,
a place of first permission,
everlasting omen of what is.
How could I not become his wife?
Just remember you are standing
on a planet that's evolving.
When I know that the grave is empty,
absence eviscerates me.
That's how it was then, a knife
through cartilage, a body broken.
In any language, a lie is a lie.
Take this dream-blown word.
Let elation be elliptical,
ecstatic carnival of fire.

Virginia Konchan

The new alphabets

The new alphabets only spell "capital."
I think my voice is being ripped from me.
I do not mean it hurts—I mean I hear the rending.
I walk to the park and toss blanched peanuts
at pigeons who scatter in terror from my gift.
I am not what you are thinking.
I am corpus and metaphysic.
I am whale bone and tendon.
I am the hitchhiker attached to my own story.
Or am I just one of Nero's soldiers,
chanting an encomium—
what choice did they have?
The crisis of conscious thought occurs
when we let elements address the body we found.
Its wholeness, its black eye and inability to sob,
was inside my closed hand.
There is an anchoress.
If someone were to photograph
the years of my life I spent young
and listening—I would not be
in the photograph at all.
When I think of you I erase most of what you say
and replace it with a courtly love poem
in the style of one of the lesser knights
following King Arthur around.
I pray mostly out of fear, some hunger.
A little dogwood tree is losing its mind.
And what I want to say is:
Give me your hands.
Give me your hands.

Kirby

"Can David Come Out to Play?"

for David Wojnarowicz

Stand behind the Rimbaud mask
he once saw the world through
Who doesn't want to be any body
even a dead boy when you're dying?

Then I see it, a piece I've only Xeroxed
so much bigger than I imagined
boy big as me ("one day this kid will
get larger") *David, I came all this way*

to see you sweet looking youth
with a museum badge in smart frames
Ask if he'll take my picture, "We're
both boys," me in my 8 Man

Baby blue tee. He smiles, I smile,
"Of course" and it hits
me full on. *David. I came
to see David.* Knees buckle

tears flood walls drop to the floor
Attendant rushes kneels beside me
strokes my back "What do you need?,"
"some water" takes my arm

leads me to another room, a bench
a window, shaded leaves I sit
Hear David's voiceover
through speakers "here,"

Kirby

he holds the glass sits with me
"Thanks" "Can I get you anything else?"
such kindness this boy
 "It's okay." "You sure? Is there someone

here with you? Can I call you a cab?"
"No really, I'll just sit here a moment,
I'll be fine" knowing nothing is
"I'm still on the floor if you need anything."

My feet return, ass meets bench
In the next room an elder male couple
also survivors sit beside one another
Hold hands watch footage unreels protests

Queers fighting for our lives dykes trans
gays always fighting for another
square inch to remain here
I ghostwalk through remains

large canvases signs paper mache
black & white nudes the new
Whitney HISTORY KEEPS ME AWAKE
AT NIGHT David's voice face eyes

Kirby

Kindness

Wait to board bus back door with pass where the walk is clear. Driver doesn't open back door. I cross ice to get to front door, slip fall hard, slide under the bus. Driver does nothing. Person boarding sees, "Wait!" Another hands me my hat,

"Are you okay, sir?"

That's exactly how it's going to happen. Last words I'll hear. A stranger politely mistaking me for sir.

Ayaz Pirani

Nakalanki

I went to the house where you were born
and it was filled with birdsong.

The rains came down and purified nothing.
Some birds cried like cats prowl.

Now when we ask for memory
we end up with a pile of men's suits.

I thought you said 3rd floor, Muhammad Ali, Karachi
but it looks more like Nakalanki's navel.

The face of a rock hopes dash on.
The swagger of interrogated nostalgia.

You made it out of the burning building.
From its touches you were born.

Ayaz Pirani

Ali's Tiger

1.

My language is abridged, thin
as a Bible's paper.

I'm trying to print
but not be two-sided.

Indifferent,
son of an owl.

Kiss me the way a plane skids.
It'll be like horses in the garden.

Or the historical disadvantage
of two grains of sand.

Ayaz Pirani

2.

How many leaves in the forest?
How many men's suits in the city?

No end to the tangles
in a guru's beard.

Ali's tiger won't let you count its stripes.
Might as well interrogate the wave.

While most words curl like leaves
I know a few the ear doesn't hear.

Are you done shaking hands with thin ice,
kissing snowdrift to snowdrift?

3.

Imagine a drawer of ornithology.
Long arms, some words.

Ayaz Pirani

Gardener

The pillows on the bed
accept each day's arrangement.

The chairs like their poses.
In the closet the broom

has its own broom.
Even the lamp enjoys its corner.

Afreen's in the garden
but it's an inquest.

Snail's on the run
for what it's done.

Stone sets
aside its feelings.

Chris Hutchinson

What I Want Isn't What I Want to Want

My life's so far behind it thinks
it's outstripping the sun. Each place replaced
by the image of a place.

My seesaw tilts to the east, then collapses
back under the weight of the present
moment's infinities.

Next, out west, the Pacific breathes and I think
I hear the colours of its tongue and throat, see the textures
of its lips as it sips the rocky shore.

Each image transfixed inside
the idea of an image. And how many of us
are just pretending?

Chris Hutchinson

Creation

A word
divides, then
the world

encroaches
and history's sparkling tide
of cruelty.

Ra becomes Zeus, then Ovid
approaches, appropriates
the entire Greek universe, etc.

Fast forward.

At this rate, the human population
will soon surpass the mass
of the entire known universe.

Wherever I am
it's always darker, brighter
wherever I'm not.

Stop.

Chris Hutchinson

Home & Garden

"Ahem," said Gorden,
and anger homed in
on his demo hanger.

"Egad," said Hermon
to the doer, Meghan,
and her game horned.

Another hard genome
and random ghee
hem groaned.

Honda merged,
hanged, and more
than hanged Rome.

At Headmen.org
the hedge manor
and an homage nerd

renamed their hog
"Hedger Noam,"
and the hog meandered,

while Meghan rode,
and Ahmed and Goren, too
back to their garden home.

Marc di Saverio

The Man with the Microchip in His Right Hand

Stopping wantless under cherry blossoms
he hears a girl singing from the sewer,
then harmonizes voices with some hums,
then sings the final chorus like he knows her,
their voices shaking red chrysanthemums—
but now the crowds of fading stars are fewer
and his voice grows weaker as the day glows nearer,
as he's alarmed by first stirs of the slums.
"Should I come up to see you on the street
so in the morning light we can now meet?"
A blossom plummets through the dewy grate.
Before he can reply I, an old class-mate,
pass by, asking why he's standing here—
"for—for cherry-trees this time of year."

Marc di Saverio

Standing on Opposite Sides of the Stream Dividing the Ravine

for Paul di Saverio

Standing on opposite sides of the stream dividing the ravine—
   you singing verses and I singing choruses, then vice-versa;
   the spring stream thin; the kindred ravine dimming;
   Mom biting her first nail on the phone with Aunt Josie;
   Dad inside the study, reciting Leopardi; both at home.
Standing on opposite sides of the stream dividing the ravine—
   you practicing your curve-balls, I catching all your curve-
   balls; we synchronized brothers with same-sized shadows,
   equal in our gifts; the strongest want each having
   for the other being that the other would out-bloom,
   out-explode him, like one cherry-blossom might out-bloom,
   out-explode another –
Standing on opposite sides of the stream dividing the ravine—
   you praying to Saint Cecile, I praying to Saint Cecile;
   the cardinals, camouflaged by the late red rays,
   seeming to shoot out of nowhere, out of the vortex
   to the reason for coincidence, the Stranger's way
   of remaining anonymous?
And, soon, telling the time by the fainting sun, I'd jump
   the stream.
And, now, I remember that holy moment when we saw how
   beautiful it'd really be, to enter our paradisal home
   before our father—in his white undershirt, young still,
   glowing unlike the sun at the ends of those evenings—
   had set out toward us.

Marc di Saverio

Sonnet of Impending Ending

I see, while teased by flower-blends in a breeze,
it's true: when we were one I could not dream
since you were all of my expectancies
arriving like this late summer moon-beam
on your body, which my eye no longer sees
as an astronomer sees the universe.
Remember when my soul lifted your curse?
When eye-lights of your blisses would high-beam
upon the earth? The balm of my tenure was hard
as death to summon, and, though love died,
I, between sleeping and waking, feel we are one
again, though we doze through nights without one
touch. I live for times I think we're still one stream—
for times I wake and still am in a dream.

Lisa Martin

ENFJ

Your heart beats thus: *with whom?* You will marry
for love, believe in good fortune, aspire.
Belonging is your art: you carry
heat, light; not fuel itself, but what sets fire.
You're a mystic, not a convert. Hyper
real. Mary Pratt with her jam jars. So: bake
a medicinal cake; change a diaper;
write this poem; leach broth from bone; learn to make
anything—light with your eyes closed, love with
them open. The whole world wants you close. Take
your time: all the best things do. You are missed.
I send letters. God's an ENFJ.

Though Christ was something else, you're God's daughter.
Leavener of spirits. Walker on the water.

Lisa Martin

INFJ

Dear friend, my first *Thou*, with you I've learned
to imagine my way to a better
place. I married a man who one day turned
away. But you'd gone ahead, sent letters
from that future: *This is your flight path. Who knows
where love goes?* I knew it would be somewhere
you'd find me. You flew, stood beside me, crows
circling overhead, too many for
that old rhyme, *one crow sorrow, two crows joy*—
You knock every form on its side. Content
to *be the beauty*, as Rumi said. Boy,
whoever wants your love better assent

to love hard, go home, touch what's shattered.
Hold it to the light. It always mattered.

Lisa Martin

INTJ

You'd light the world if we could just hook up
your brain to an energy-efficient
bulb. Like one of those bicycles, y'know? Yup,
you're electric, but quietly: proficient
in just about everything. You pride your-
self on that. But God knows you're the greatest
risk she's ever taken: you don't suffer,
nor look twice, having searched once. Atheist
by temperament, a fine irony, since
you do your ontology the way you
once did me: with your armour on—don't wince—
swelled lobes. Not present with your whole being.

You're certain of this: you'll solve, in your life,
one of the great problems. And love your wife.

Matthew Walsh

Bliss

At fifteen my true love came to me, the internet,
with my own email address, where I felt safe,

grounded, watching a homosexual cowboy download
on dial-up while giving me the tip of his hat, waiting

for myself to figure out I would never be that type of man,
instinctive already in me was the ability to build up

a cocoon of sweater and layers to hibernate like a computer.
The shadow on my upper lip, my mother was dead

set my father would teach me in the mirror to shave
my face, this was before I had discovered Lacan—

regardless I had no trust in the male gender or body
image. Later in life I am glad to avoid the mirror—

I had an ocean where I saw enough, further, and later came
to places where water appeared to meet sky like the travel

commercials foretold, but they left out the bliss of disorientation
in seeing the world where you can't tell ocean from sky,

and yet I waded out regardless, into the simple color blue
up north in Shippigan, not knowing clam from star.

Matthew Walsh

Soft Core

It is hard to admit to myself that I have a life in this body
when sometimes I feel my life is long enough.

My past I drank to create my own cinema, a black screen
in my head, to remember not one dream, my brain

a powered-down TV. I wish I could have let it be known
that I was queer earlier in my memory, without the years

of strange anguish with no name, and sad, independent
films about coming to terms with homosexuals,

or gays succumbing to AIDS. I remember hiding who I was I was
terrified and used to think that there was no gay cinema

until I watched a soft core porn titled *Boyfriends*
late at night, the tide at its lowest, the moon high and okay.

I had never seen this before, the moment my desires
were on screen like this, an on-screen kiss, then anal

and my mistake was accepting opinion of others
to be true when the only true thing is I am living.

Matthew Walsh

Iamb

I have made it hard to see myself as anything other
than a fat depressed person who just wants to recover

what I lost. Acceptance is so tough. If I wear purple
my friend calls me Grimace, from the Kingdom of McDonald's

or allegorically, Purple Dick (kingdom unknown).
This kind of language only brings me to a new height

in body dysmorphia where I am comfortable telling my joke:
What is the loneliest thing on earth? Iamb.

I realized that I found my people much later in life
and that I can make choices for myself, like I used to

go to parties and beg my straight friends not to say I'm gay,
worried that I would be a pair of novelty chattery teeth,

wound up, questioned about why I'm not more, like, flamboyant,
be pulled, like, an ocean into a freezer room by a drunk boyfriend.

What I'm saying is: I would have liked to have lived how
I wanted without becoming any type of man.

Khashayar "Kess" Mohammadi

Ghazal 14

Fariduddin Attar (1145-1221 AD)

who is the augur in our company tonight
whose face illuminates humanity tonight

no flicker to the candle, no sparkle from the moon
not even the morning star seems shiny tonight

in our company a face so brilliant such that
the sun hides from shame and courtesy tonight

much happiness shall come from this night forth
since Jupiter and Venus align in harmony tonight

a blessed night with no strangers in the midst
being among loved ones means much glory tonight

tonight no one comes in between me and you
there's a calm retreat in our privacy tonight

let the bard compose from these fits of excitement
a song to celebrate the lovers' festivity tonight

all is a pleasant tale of Attar's sorrow
this sweet song the bard's singing tonight

Khashayar "Kess" Mohammadi

Ghazal 441

Mevlana Jalaluddin Muhammad Rumi (1207-1273 AD)

show face, it is flowers and greenery that I seek
open lips, it is sweetness and sugar that I seek

O sun of virtue! come out from behind the clouds
it is that brilliant, twinkling, radiant visage that I seek

flirtatiously you said "don't bother me anymore. just leave"
it is that tone of "don't bother me anymore" that I seek

and one time hearing "leave! since the king is not home"
it is blunt confrontation with the royal guard that I seek

I swear to Allah, this city is a prison without you
it is nomadic wandering in the deserts and the mountains that I seek

disappointed from all these weak-willed companions
it is the Lion of God and Rostam of Dastan that I seek

the heart wilts from the Pharaoh and his tyranny
it is the radiant visage of the prophet Moses that I seek

I've grown tired of the constant nagging of commonfolk
it is drunken roars, it is cacophony that I seek

I'm more eloquent than the nightingale, but from rampant envy
my mouth is sealed shut, it is Afghanistan that I seek

yesterday the Sheikh roamed the streets with a lantern
that "I'm tired of beasts and demons, it is the human that I seek"

they said "the human can't be found, we've searched all"
Sheikh said "it is that which cannot be found that I seek"

Khashayar "Kess" Mohammadi

no matter how destitute I am, I will not accept common stone
it is that cheap. yet rare diamond that I seek

absent from all vision, yet all vision is from God
it is that evident mystery of absence that I seek

my ears heard the story of faith and became inebriated
which virtue of vision? it is the face of faith that I seek

one hand a wine vessel, the other entangled in the hair of the beloved
it is this dance amidst the town square that I seek

the famous Shams of Tabriz, show face from the East
I'm the Hoopoe, it is the company of Sulayman that I seek

Simina Banu

from *harmony in Beach Foam*

I'm not as excited about sanding
as I used to be. Dust.
Dancing. I'm not as excited
about solos. I never expected twenty-eight
to be nothing. The card expired.
The coffee's cold.
It's true that I dropped my anxiety
ring into the risotto again—careful.
Whatever, I guess I'll buy some garbage bags.
The cashier smiles when she sees my sandcastle mold,
not knowing I will be using it to mix water into a phosphate-free degreaser.

*

There's more paint on the floors than the walls.

The neighbour's dog killed my favourite daffodil.

This lightbulb could depress a ukulele.

Simina Banu

*

I limbo so hard
that I'm actually just lying down now.
S450-1 Beach Foam
laps at my toes.
I killed the vibe, so
the cellar spider politely exits the room.
What was there
before foam?
(Note: that's spackling on my face
but why?)

*

I can't pronounce anesthetist.
I don't comb my hair
because the plants survive
regardless. The ants
haven't colonized. The mold's benign.

Simina Banu

*

Desperate to move,
I listen to a podcast.
I realize beach foam is fine
but what about

    red

    and red

    and red
    and

*

Despite hating food,
I try to swallow my heart.
It's a little too high.
A cartoon thief
on the ceiling
as I inspect the commotion.

Simina Banu

*

and red is what matisse painted his harmony
in blue

the spider's back
looking for trouble so
i put down the paint roller

my coats
peeling anyway
i wonder what there was before
red before

foam
before

Blair Trewartha

Half-Earth

Heat was a soft glove wrapping your lungs.
We bathed you in a pool of melting snow,
palms cradling your back, your belly
breaching like an ice cube in the sun.
All around us, firestorms. Something
like an animal scraping forest-ward.
She was there, and then not there,
so you and I burned our years like lost
dogs until one day my hand felt your forehead
and there was instant—fearful, sober.
At dusk, you first waved to me. I told you
of a town where rooftops keep people alive,
where billboards drink air and quench thirst,
where everyone grasps the heavy weight
of forest die back, the infernal range
of the bell curve and how we fool ourselves
every time. With your first step, I taught you
to swim, how to hold someone's hand
as you shove your palm into their chest,
how skin burns with or without a belief
in flame. With your first word, you asked me
what we had known before and I said
everything. All of it. We let it anchor
to the pendulum as it swung, tried to predict
the landing, calculate the gap
between two right angles, argued
whether it should have ever swung at all.

Blair Trewartha

Modern American Worship

after Geoffrey Morrison's "Two Diaries"

There's no such thing as small blessings:
an optimist's clever way of taking punches
and sucking it up. Clarity. Gratefulness.
Words of prayer squeezed through a rosary
of scabbed fists. Bad news never comes
without its antithesis. America: a hunter
who thinks it's a lion—chasing its tail.

When God gives you lemons, there is no God.
Pucker up. Eat fruit. Pretend there's no such
thing as a wound self-inflicted. At the initial
kneel, that mercy-drunk monologue
with eyes shut and pleading, we became
conquerors believing they were worshippers
doing someone else's will. Five hundred

years of frigid rain is still a void of drought.
In the wars of water, we'll wield an arsenal.
Any land that can't be burned is just a fire
You let us put out. This is the wisdom
of worshippers: word reversals
and resuscitations. A way to pull
the slaughter out of the blade after the cut.

Triny Finlay

Livewire

> *I love a wild fountain's clear gush in a gully in a squall*
> *secreted within its headlands my caress*
>
> *if this tiny despair-basket I lead with were real*
> *it would be of woven willow*
> —Phil Hall, *Killdeer*

I love the peppers you fire in cast iron, shishitos,
one in every ten or so a livewire.
I love the notes you fire off to me, filling
me in on the vast inscape of your day-to-day.
I love the giant bed we share, a hot zone for sex, safe
for sleep for cease-fires for writing out fears.
I love the mushy bananas you grind into soft-
serve, our dairy-free treat in high summer,
melting melting like my lips on your molten mouth.
I love a wild fountain's clear gush in a gully in a squall

in an asbestos-ridden hallway on campus:
it's still water, still a gush, still the thing I need
for relief right then and there. I love the way
you cup each hand against my back, moving
up like a snail, leaving the trace of a touch-trail.
I love the jerk and pull of you, your perfect teeth
so tender as they nip and tug at my skin. I love
the slow build-up to a roar: we're tigers in the sheets,
turtles in the streets. I love your throaty tenor,
secreted within its headlands my caress

Triny Finlay

as if my body could bring it out of you without
touching. I love your twice-licked finger flicking
through the pages of a much-loved book,
Archie alongside Winterson, Foucault.
I love your crisp dress shirts that arrive by mail
as if sent by a private tailor, whom I imagine big, queer,
and attracted—like bee to honeysuckle—to scent, to flair.
I love your meticulous scrutiny: of menus, of theories,
of freckles and moles, of food magazines. And
if this tiny despair-basket I lead with were real

enough to gather up our traumas; if we were weaker
than those blistered shishitos; if our hands were colder
than the shoulders of former friends; if our meals
were just white bread with the crusts cut off; if so, then we
wouldn't be who we are right now, this minute:
together, the sun-smacked glow of our forearms matched
after a day at L'Aboiteau, belting out Peaches
in the car: *Just keep it going. Just keep it going.* No hurricane
should loosen this love, for it is a force now, as strong as
it would be of woven willow.

Triny Finlay

We Cannot Be Contained

after Maja Padrov's pottery

Do not discount the alchemy, do not overlook
what makes the potter's body shift and gaze.
Lip, neck, shoulder, belly, foot,

but most of all her hands, the rut
they scrape and gash in stoneware clays.
Do not discount the alchemy. Do not overlook

this chance realm of interlocking spires, each rook
dipped and fired in red iron or cobalt oxide glaze.
Lip, neck, shoulder, belly, foot—

we want to see ourselves in everything: put
birth marks on fruit bowls, pour our own blood in the vase.
Do not discount the alchemy, do not overlook

this perfect chain of shape and time and soot,
a romance with the kiln, its stable blaze.
Lip, neck, shoulder, belly, foot,

but most of all her hands, the way they took
to earth, as if to garden: soil fills her days.
Do not discount the alchemy; do not overlook
lip, neck, shoulder, belly, foot.

Darren Bifford

Purgatory

for my daughter

It is a disputed doctrine.

Unlike hellfire and damnation, scriptural support is lacking.

Yet on a weekend we wander the halls of a hospital ward and encounter no one.

It's only later I recall that the nurse wore plain clothes, winter boots, drank a coffee to-go.

The clearest evidence is the existence of a windowless room, its tiny locked door.

One arrives there by finding oneself already sitting there.

Invariably there's a moment when one recalls having forgotten to ask how long the wait will be.

It's no use beating oneself up about that.

I suspect this characteristic of what it is thus to wait.

As every cause is an effect of a prior cause, and so on.

The place of rest is where-ever you've happened for the time being to collapse.

Pacing suggests there is some question one has not resolved. Or, for that matter, asked.

No, turns out there are a few others present. I note a father on his phone a few seats over.

The desire to talk is impossible to fulfill. In that respect it is like every other desire.

Darren Bifford

I've asked about how long we're scheduled to wait. How long the operation will be.

I mean- I've written a note to remind myself later not to forget to ask.

If, that is, anyone official turns up.

Also characteristic is rudderless worry and ubiquitous fear.

Yet I'm told neither to worry nor give way to fear.

By 'told' I mean that I read that advice somewhere once.

It should be but it is not is a common refrain. *Unfortunately* is another.

Need not be but is is what I say, recollecting my edition of Aurelius' *Meditations*.

Now here's something you won't believe:

Not far, a little boy—no, a girl!—runs our way through the hall

silently and very fast.

Darren Bifford

Paradise

The argument runs roughly as follows: all desire is wayward.
We misunderstand ourselves. What we desire turns old, incomplete.

What we desire is not what we meant by desiring. What did I mean?

I found myself saying I wished to love more than what the body wants.
If also I am flesh, let that go without question.

. . .

Every day I fall in love, said Jim, the painter, some years before he died.
Beauty is not thrifty.

Every day Jim painted what he loved, all the light turning in on things,
the rooftops, trees, all the bodies without faces turning in upon one another

as if some beach beside some blue sea extends far within us and around us.

. . .

Jan is always pressing her hand to her heart;
her mouth expresses what astonishment looks like in still-life.

She turns toward the waterfall at the head of some trail
so that all I see looking at her is the back of her head.

. . .

Though I hear nothing, though the sound is the sound of an electric light,
there is a real westerly light passing through the window of her office.

Despair presumes too much.

It shines on all the colours of the spines of all the books she's unpacked
to fill the shelves of the wall above her desk. My mouth must hang open,

Darren Bifford

untutored, because she said she can see all my desire all at once
by the way I look at all those books stacked across her shelves.

Despair presumes that it means what it says.

· · ·

It is not the smell of the girl who I wished for ten years so much to fuck
because she would never give herself to me and because I'd never asked.

What was her name? No, I knew her name.
She told me.

That was how I called her when I wanted her.

· · ·

All desire is wayward, desire cruel. That's the old argument.
So in the lower levels of hell the souls without a body are nonetheless

stuck to one another, their desire revealed to them:
this is what you really wanted. Look at it forever.

· · ·

Tell me something now.
If I never leave home again, will that be permanence?

What I believe seems so silly. After a near eternity of climbing,
over a few documented days, I too will stand at the edge of a wall of fire

outlining the lost garden. Inside, in a dress made of red,
my daughter will stand waiting as she is in her fifth year, inviolable.

All my fear overwhelmed by a love not made restless
by division and indisposition. Let me skin myself and stretch

Darren Bifford

. . .

my skin so that the pain doesn't pass through it. The world flush and rebuffed.
My children hidden. Ah, if only. But the desire to make the welter calm,

to calm the crowd all worked up for some trivial reason. To sit quiet awhile.
To hold her small hand in my hand and pull her in the direction of her school.

Sarah Burgoyne

Instructions for Recognition

Your arm must follow the flight of balloons to a silver trumpet suspended in air.

You must pull it down and blow to awaken the danceless, shaped as mannequins.

The gesture upsets ~~Time's~~ Capital's dialectic.

Dance it.

There were entities that were powered through breath or wind, were mechanical and then appeared living to the people viewing them.

Film the dance in gown-surround.

Be ornate jellyfish in a glass pond.

Be the glass pond's accidental passante.

The accident is your only alignment.

History is an accident.

Let it enter as an automaton to dance alongside.

History's royal ~~body~~ bodies are rigid and put on gowns.

A procession of balloons' twist from the sky.

The scene (in Time's aquarium) is without smell, but a wreath encircles a missing eye.

History has shaped the heads without giving them orifices.

These are its faces: bald, sightless queens glistening in plastic skin.

Above them is the photograph of the Real.

Sarah Burgoyne

Your reflection fills the aquarium as does snow's ghost.

As the Dancer and History, be both somewhere and nowhere.

Be injected with night.

Time faints (at least how we knew it).

Dance like water.

Beneath plastic leaves, become a tree.

Become the stump.

Send out power and trace it, smiling.

If the passante starts to run, run also.

Disco the Plaza by throwing its light around.

Hop to and fro.

Your ~~body~~ bodies sea-spray to tree.

The sea spray takes a moment to hang stars in the air before hiding them behind its back.

The passantes, whose faces hang still as droplets in the video, for a moment, are yours.

Use the dance to reveal that the first videowork was a river.

History is a river stone, smoothed by time.

You may think of time as the constant movement in one direction but use the dance to show this is not time's way.

Mime its cliché.

Sarah Burgoyne

Then point to its rupture.

The idea of a moving body—that's not real or organic—is an old idea, but I feel like we're off topic anyway.

The poles that hold up the awning mimic the tree, so hug them.

The Plaza itself is a kind of cyborg.

Let the snow gently press your voice to the ground.

Listen to the snow say there are many meanings to the word "temps."

In time and weather, women are no longer pawns of capitalism but appendages of the cyborg.

Coincidentally, it is five o'clock and cloudy.

It's part of the spectacle of commerce that you're drawn to the window, and you're looking at the commercial object, then you imagine yourself making it move.

Climb the air, but do not mistake this for progress.

Don't forget the awning stretches above you.

In the dance, be a crane that moves backwards, fainting into a pond.

All arms are archways, or drawbridges, transhumanists replacing parts of their bodies, like the Neoliberal sense of gentrification and commerce above all else.

How (on earth) to move on the earth without damage.

Make a decision.

Be a mime who pulls down the weather.

Cut thunder across your ~~body~~ bodies.

Sarah Burgoyne

The grey clouds dangle their wrists.

Limpness wipes the brow of sky.

To use a space in a way you're not meant to makes History perform a runway spin and faint.

March with fullness now, in sudden uniform.

The poles hold up the sky.

The bench holds up the ground.

Lean back and stroke air's fur.

The five fingers of five o'clock reach into the sky, so you can hold its object which is dusk light.

"Entre le chien et le loup."

The new passante is self-conscious.

The pole spins the storm and you.

Spin an embrace.

What words live here?

History slides down to rise again and this is the negative image.

Knock to find the exit.

But be baffled by its mechanical newness.

The observers are plastic and therefore frozen without temperature.

Shake it off to enter warmth.

Sarah Burgoyne

Arms are gowns you flow down.

A coat is for wing-making.

Perform the skip of fantasy.

The automaton is freely moving; it doesn't require a buyer, but it does require that you buy into the fantasy.

Perform the purchase of fantasy.

Dance the circumference of a dress.

Be its fullness.

You are trying to make palpable something that disappears into error—I mean air—you know, and then is gone.

Time's head spins.

Its hands flip and fold.

You are under trial, but accept it.

An eye levels to your eye.

A leading with the wrists equals politesse.

Spin into the Now.

The women without faces both watch and never watch.

The snow is much more understanding.

Pressing the hand to cold metal presses the body to the cold.

Knock a few times there.

Sarah Burgoyne

Shake it off.

Gown your arms.

Gown the mind.

Kick.

Make an ad for nothing.

Encircle the detritus as though it's sacred.

It is.

Where does History look?

The people approach.

The glass reflects their ghosts.

Their ghosts' footsteps stutter to a stop.

Matt Rader

Atmospheric Moon River

December loomed

with its supply chain of moods

The plum tree's last medallions of golden leaves

its rivière of blue

light emitting diodes for Diwali

In my dreams

I could do no violence. No matter how

hard I tried

I'd no force to execute my attacks

I stomped

dream body after dream body

but no one

was ever hurt

as if something wanted

to remind me, even in my sleep

of my impotence

in global affairs, as if something wanted

to save me. *Westron wynde when wyll thow blow*

Matt Rader

I listened

to *In a Sentimental Mood*

nightly. I borrowed a distinction between porn

and pornography

Mornings, the moon lowered itself

over the western mountains

and hung there

golden white

against the sky's cool complexion

not even looking at me

but looking at me

if you know what I mean. *Tomorrow*

sex will be good again

is a phrase I read

and repeated via text to a colleague

working on affect theory

in Hungary

a person

for whom I had indeterminate feelings

Matt Rader

Psychic excess

they called it

quoting

Judith Butler Yeats

On the other side of the mountains

a thin river of water

poured like grief through the atmosphere

wiping out everything

bridges, hillsides, farmland

Only debt survived

barely

I got to thinking

how that cameo moon might look on me

with my undertones

of firebush and raspberry

my cobalt

disbelief in money

the thin tremulous needle of futurity

that fluttered

Matt Rader

in all my poetry. I was in an elevator

ascending a glass tower

the floor numbers lighting up

like cigarettes

in the dark, like parts of my brain

when I sang

the smalle rayne downe can Rayne. Across the province

we gathered

candles and sandbags

We prepared

to lose all

power

Above the building

beyond the many panels of tempered glass

a tower crane floated

in the river

of rain. Even then we knew abundance

Autumn's harvest

of darkness

Matt Rader

in which tiny green lights grew

like mushrooms

along the jib of the crane

Cryst yf my love were in my Armys

And I yn my bed Agayne

I heard

the wind sing

There's no such thing

as an aesthetic death mudslide

Atmospheric moon river

I'm crossing you

Angela Hibbs

Power

Why have a body?

Measure the distance from the sun to the clouds. Be that far
and that dominant.

The fun in love is predicting how it will end. The sky won't let
anyone break up with it.
Clouds take orders: replay highlight reels; brag best formations; disturb sleep.

The sky leads, misleads: a beautiful spouse whose beauty dries up.
Silent treat. Punish into humility.

Or, of course, the sky — familiar only with the present
tense — is unmarried.
Consider every night a divorce.

The sky invents immortality.
Flee when a companion
claims loyalty, if
not long before.

All impressions are biochemical. The unforgettable is beyond control.
I am the sky I am the why the unnameable and this is my shadow.

Angela Hibbs

Plot Points

Who is more innocent
than MacBeth's witches?

Serket protects
removed contents:
the liver to the south;
stomach: east; intestines: west; lungs: north.

Refrain from unravelling intestines.
Human, jackal, baboon,
falcon; each guard canopic jars.
The organs may be retrieved

as needed. A prince needs
to scale Rapunzel's prison spire. She's picking her hair with a distaff
an evil fairy cursed. This familiar setting is not a trap.
This gothic spire awaits a villain's trip.

Snow White was accustomed to meringue piled like clouds.
Bumping her head on door frames at the Little People's cottage, their food
left her hungry. Here, a witch's palmed fruit offered satisfaction.
The witch's eyes: familiar.

Eat the whole apple, even the stem.

Angela Hibbs

The Ocean's Bookie

The moon is no messenger.
Whose view is broader than the sky's? It doesn't breathe a word.
Nobody volunteers to be an ocean.

Body counts are fine but how missed are these people?
Fewer newspapers hit the ocean than ever before.
Nobody reads obituaries there.

No mirror for the ocean. Tosses practiced
on shores without skin
in the game. Earthquakes are shrugs, tsunamis just a sneeze.

Nobody asked the Ocean if it wanted to be ridden, written.
The Earth steals the Ocean's thunder one more time.

Sure, Godzilla may be in the belly. Braggers at gambling tables.
How did the Ocean get hired? Hasn't it been replaced by the sky:

its efficient travel; its pollution often invisible?
The Ocean wave, ready to do battle. How did the Pacific look last week?

These birds take forever and forget more than they knew.
The ocean challenges the sky to the hurricane-tsunami off.

Bike racks at lunch time.
Rain trespasses.

Star crossed fighters: star fish versus stars.
Albatross versus abalone.

Algae. Amberjack. Anglerfish.
Reclaim it all; keep the vocabulary.

Janette Platana

The Literacy Fairy

Literacy dwells, ubiquitous, in every mark
made to stand for sound and meaning,
noiselessly knelling your cranial bell
with Her invisible,
audible, visceral
tonguing.

She is the counter to claims
of earthy fabrication,
origination,
and celestial prestidigitation.

Soil and water are well and holy
but without this mystery
we are mere strutting, fucking, squawking, mobile
mud.

She alters consciousness.

I summon and supplicate
with each scribble, each stroke,
thumbed or typed; you pray
no matter when or where,
nor proximal nor apart.
Our co-creation,
unconfined by ark or time,
covenants this wonder.

To read and write is a gasping miracle
misidentified, mistaken, misdefined,
but unshakeably divine.
It is enough. It is enough.

Janette Platana

The Fairies Reify & Deify

They are not twins, these two,
but reciprocating parasites who

refuse to play host.
Yet each outstrips the other

in unxious luxury. Sheets and pillows (smother
smother) make them dream

of lovers' lovers as they stifle petit-
mort cries, little forkings.

Jacknife bodies tine together,
pricks renuded, smooth as windchimes.

Impossible to pinpoint
who came first, they start again

and you join them with your eyes closed,
automatic. Reify makes abstract real,

while Deify, their lover,
sits and watches.

We are gods for that short
moment. Like velveteen rabbits,

rubbing makes us real,
leaves us raw by the effort.

Janette Platana

The Second Coming of The Yeats Fairy

Falconer, falcon:
viewed from above, at the cliff's brim, neither
seems to carry much conviction.
The lake drains in a narrowing
gyre, counter to the wisdom of clocks.

Soften those loosening thighs.
Is that a feather?
Sharpen your quill.
This Fairy likes a smooth beast.

Coasting the thermals, the falcon rises;
something is let go; it drops:
passion, compassion.
Release your prey and hope for the best.

The splash – a crown in the water – fulfills all its purposes
in an instant
for an instant:
ripples increase in number, increase in size and velocity
as they race away from the site,
fleeing gleefully to shore.

Pluck. Shave. Smooth your hair. Tie your cravat. Stand up straight. You are a lion of a man.
Get ready
to be born.

Douglas Walbourne-Gough

Orange

Orange will take your face and shake
your cheeks without warning,
muss your hair before casually
walking away. Orange has a bad tattoo,
waters its plants with Grand Marnier.

Orange likes the idea of romance,
but would rather you didn't overthink it.
Orange is proficient in tai chi
and lawn darts. Double-dips guacamole
without apology and gooses you at church.

Orange will always owe you money
and never fail to remind you *ain't nothin'*
that rhymes with me, dollface.
You'll place another twenty in its hand
before realizing it's hopeless. You're in love.

Douglas Walbourne-Gough

Red

Blood and guts of course; poppies;
roses; how serious sentiment
can come by bouquet. Raw meat
and the kiss it leaves on the butcher's block.
Scarlet patent leather shoes.

Red is self-explanatory. Hopelessly
devoted to loving the ideal, it's the lip-
sticked pig yearning to be kissed
into a prince. Red embraces cliché,
cries all the way through *All Dogs Go to Heaven*,

mistakenly calls its teacher Mom.
Red is also an alarm, hell's truest hue,
is liquid geology bursting forth to forever
alter our landscape, the coals of every dying fire.
Red the heart, too big to be denied.

Douglas Walbourne-Gough

Purple

for Kaila Ruth

Your dad's old fleece jacket,
the way you say it fits my waist,
broadens my shoulders; makes
me strut. Proudly imbued
with its royal hue, with your trust.

Or, more suited to you, lilacs.
Their late-June scent, how they
send me sauntering up your street,
my body abuzz with knowing
it'll fall asleep next to yours.

Violet, how it carries so much blue,
yet never feels heavy with it.
A field of soft edges, bees coming
and going. I watch, humbled
by so many pairs of wings at work.

Remember that time a kid was selling
chunks of amethyst on Duckworth,
and you were in St. Pierre? I whispered
tu me manques to every small rock I saw,
cursed Signal Hill for its silence.

The subtle silk of your skin's shift
against mine, its aubergine
a rush of hot blood rousing my mouth
to your neck, your voice midnight plum
as we find our fervent niche.

Jenna Lyn Albert

mal à l'aise

1.

dans le rêve je suis serpentine, naked and coiled around a clutch of eggs
the cream colour of magnolias or a plume of oyster mushrooms. nestled
in the cathedral-hollow of an ancient oak, a rash of ochre lichen blooms
over my skin: too many moons have passed with no visible change,
no signs of pipping—sole comfort the vascular webs and embryos
made visible by candling each egg to sun. the litterfall cannot sustain
us come autumn, oblong shells clotted tightly together for insulation.

2.

as *sage-femme* I bite-tear into the shells delicately, membranes tough
yet malleable as untreated leather. one by one, each sheath gives way
to teeth—scrying the hagstones I see nothing. unsteady fingers blunt
dissect primordial ooze, find no foeti or yolk or amorphous viscera—

                                        only the translucent goo of
                            speculum lubricant
                    ultrasound jelly
            cervical mucus
    semen

3.

aménorrhée, I have been unable to shed for months—abdomen
constricting ceaselessly. menses in retrograde, I chew chicory root.
romance the stone. repeat ritual after ritual to coax my body
from brumation. no amount of palpation, of prodding brings on
a blood. the nest's remnants have been scavenged or released
to the earth, fungi and fauna knowing your taste—carrion.

Jenna Lyn Albert

floriography I

in the box of teacups there's a cross-stitch just shy of finished:
wild pansies with indigo petals joined in a butterscotch pucker.

rose passed before I could share that I am a florist of sorts.
had she known all who were welcome to my flower bed

would she have embraced me still? had she known about
the *plant lady* embroidered tea towel, how I'd removed the y

with a seam ripper because lad felt more neutral, more natural
somehow, would she have weeded the pansy from her garden?

what ifs are perennial. what if we close that book, preserve
what was as it was like I'd done with the sympathy flowers—

prone to crumbling and not quite the same, but keepsake.

Jenna Lyn Albert

so who does what during, you know?

after Chen Chen's "Zombie Kindnesses"

my partner is Christ, newly resurrected
and I the incredulous Thomas: gently
feeling the opening in their side
with a single finger first, then two—
coaxing the flesh tenderly until my
fist can fully penetrate the holy ghost.
the same way you come up against
the cervix if you go deep enough,
you can feel the throbbing of the heart,
can clasp your hand around the wriggling
kitten of it and experience the skip,
that little death that comes from true
ecstasy: is it so hard to imagine what
two bodies can do with one another now?

MICHAEL CHANG

SPECIAL SNOOZE

        When u tell me abt ur experience on the train
w/ the Congressional "helper"

        I start to laugh
partly b/c the correct term is *staffer*

        partly b/c I don't want to admit that I am happy
in case it gets taken away from me

        —this happiness emanating from our general vicinity
So I shut my mouth, careful not to show teeth

        The same way I suppose tribes of animals
tend to be mindful of when they bare their fangs

        if the gods are watching
I'm not allowed to be too happy

        I'm not sure why I think this
Probably something learned from television

        specifically The Mentalist on CBS
where I noticed that Harry Styles has the exact same face

        as River Phoenix
All I know is:

        There will be hell to pay
for our reckless disregard

        not necessarily for the truth
But for our shared circumstances

MICHAEL CHANG

LOW-KEY HIT OF THE SUMMER

The best & worst in New Yorkers comes out whenever anybody asks *What train goes to Times Square?*

●

Poets love to court sleep (what is sleep)

●

We haven't forgotten what color the "flesh" crayon is

●

U bulge profanely

●

A smooth oblong

●

Glans like a merman's

●

Sillage of fine fragrance, always noticed

●

Drill life into me

●

I want the #13

MICHAEL CHANG

-

- No #13 but I can give u #12 & upcharge u

-

- We pay too much

-

- With inflation #13 is now #14

-

- I lie still, think of nothing

-

- Enough trouble on my own, I could suck u in

Anstruther Checklist

Chapbooks

2014

- ☐ Jess Taylor – *Never Stop*
- ☐ Shane Neilson – *We Need Our Names*
- ☐ Richard Kelly Kemick – *Pyrrhic*

2015

- ☐ Jessica Popeski – *The Wrong Place*
- ☐ Chris Banks – *Invaders*
- ☐ Josh Stewart – *Temptation as a Technical Difficulty*
- ☐ Novelette Munroe – *…of a Wingless Woman*
- ☐ Marc di Saverio – *Death Calls*
- ☐ Christine Minnery – *Better*
- ☐ Allison LaSorda – *Playdate*
- ☐ Klara du Plessis – *Wax Lyrical*
- ☐ Bardia Sinaee – *Blue Night Express*
- ☐ Kayla Czaga – *Enemy of the People*
- ☐ Jessica Popeski – *Oratorio*

2016

- ☐ Brooke Carter – *Poco Loco*
- ☐ Asa Boxer and David-Antoine Williams – *Etymologies*
- ☐ David Alexander – *Modern Warfare*
- ☐ Aaron Boothby – *Reperspirations, Exhalations, and Wrapt Inflections*
- ☐ Aidan Chafe – *The Sharpest Tooth*
- ☐ Conor Mc Donnell – *The Book of Retaliations*
- ☐ Geneviève Robichaud – *Exit Text*
- ☐ Laura Ritland – *Marine Science*
- ☐ Ruth Roach Pierson – *Untranslatable Thought*
- ☐ Rebecca Salazar – *Guzzle*
- ☐ Jeff Latosik – *Helium Ear*
- ☐ Andy Verboom – *Tower*
- ☐ Dani Couture – *Black Sea Nettle*

2017

- ☐ Chad Campbell – *Euphonia*
- ☐ Jenny Haysom – *Blinding Afternoons*
- ☐ Curtis LeBlanc – *Good for Nothing*
- ☐ T. Liem – *Tell Everybody I Say Hi*
- ☐ Neil Surkan – *Super, Natural*
- ☐ Shazia Hafiz Ramji – *Prosopopoeia*
- ☐ Darren Bifford – *The Age of Revolution*
- ☐ Stephanie Davidson – *Go Blind*
- ☐ Krischan Stotz – *Brother Magnet*
- ☐ S. Takatsu – *Kawatare*
- ☐ Ally Fleming – *The Worst Season*
- ☐ Stewart Cole – *Alien Freight*
- ☐ Dawid Koloszyc – *The Lives of Barbarians*
- ☐ Emily Skov-Nielsen – *Volta*
- ☐ R.P. LaRose – *A Dream in the Bush*
- ☐ David Ly – *Stubble Burn*

2018

- ☐ Jade Wallace – *Rituals of Parsing*
- ☐ Lily Wang – *Everyone in Your Dream is You*
- ☐ Erin Hiebert – *Save Our Crowns*
- ☐ Mark Laliberte – *asemanticasymmetry*
- ☐ James Lindsay – *Ekphrasis! Ekphrasis!*
- ☐ Evan Jones – *The Drawing, The Ship, The Afternoon*
- ☐ James Arthur – *Hundred Acre Wood*
- ☐ Paola Ferrante – *The True Confessions of Buffalo Bill*
- ☐ Fawn Parker – *Weak Spot*
- ☐ David Groulx – *Am A Skin Too*

Chapbooks

- [ ] Amy LeBlanc – *Ladybird, Ladybird*
- [ ] Andrew Brooks – *One Country After*
- [ ] Emily Osborne – *Biometrical*
- [ ] Anton Pooles – *Monster 36*
- [ ] J.M. Francheteau – *Heart & Mouth & Deed & Life*

2019

- [ ] Jacqueline Bourque – *The Dune as Bookmark*
- [ ] Oubah Osman – *Hereditary Blue*
- [ ] Manahil Bandukwala – *Paper Doll*
- [ ] Eugenia Zuroski – *Hovering, Seen*
- [ ] Aaron Tucker – *Catalogue D'Oiseaux*
- [ ] Jaclyn Desforges – *Hello Nice Man*
- [ ] Jason Purcell – *A Place More Hospitable*
- [ ] David Barrick – *Incubation Chamber*
- [ ] Mélanie-Christine Lefebvre – *Birds Have Started to Fly into Windows Again*
- [ ] Virginia Konchan – *The New Alphabets*
- [ ] Andreae Callanan – *Crown*
- [ ] Matea Kulić – *Paperwork*
- [ ] C.L. Johnson – *culminate/knot*
- [ ] Tolu Oloruntoba – *Manubrium*
- [ ] Terese Mason Pierre – *Surface Area*

2020

- [ ] rob mclennan – *Anstruther, a history*
- [ ] Ellen Chang Richardson – *Unlucky Fours*
- [ ] Carl Watts – *Originals*
- [ ] Alison Braid-Fernandez – *Little Hunches*
- [ ] Samuel Strathman – *In Flocks of Three to Five*
- [ ] Ayaz Pirani – *Bachelor of Art*
- [ ] Marc Perez – *Borderlands*

- [ ] Síle Englert – *The Phobic's Handbook*
- [ ] Mahaila Smith – *Claw Machine*
- [ ] Kirby – *What Do You Want to Be Called?*
- [ ] Ian Pople – *Spillway*
- [ ] Benjamin C. Dugdale – *Saint Rat O'Sphere's Formica Canticle Poems*
- [ ] Tracy Wai de Boer – *maybe, basically*
- [ ] Mark Callanan – *Skylarking*
- [ ] Claire Farley – *Bait & Switch*
- [ ] Franco Cortese – *Timē Soð*
- [ ] Elizabeth Mudenyo – *With Both Hands*
- [ ] Alisha Dukelow – *Pareidolia*

2021

- [ ] Julian Day – *Late Summer Flowers*
- [ ] Daniel Beauregard – *Total Darkness Means No Notifications*
- [ ] Victoria Mbabazi – *chapbook*
- [ ] Asha Jeffers – *Mundane, Majestic*
- [ ] Chris Hutchinson – *Meanwhile, Myrmidons*
- [ ] Marc di Saverio – *Aftersongs*
- [ ] Lisa Martin – *Typology*
- [ ] Void Nason – *liquid birth*
- [ ] Matthew Walsh – *ICQ*
- [ ] Gary Barwin – *The Human Body*
- [ ] Jessica Le – *The Nearest Sweetest Thing*
- [ ] Amanda Merpaw – *Put the Ghosts Down Between Us*
- [ ] Nick Thran – *The Cloud from All Sides*
- [ ] Khashayar "Kess" Mohammadi – *The Divine Bergamot*
- [ ] Patrick Grace – *Dastardly*
- [ ] Shane Neilson – *For the Living*

Chapbooks

2022

- ☐ Joseph Kidney – *Terra Firma, Pharma Sea*
- ☐ Breanna Ho – *Uncharted*
- ☐ Sarah Teitel – *Nesting Doll*
- ☐ Simina Banu – *harmony in Beach Foam*
- ☐ Michael Caesar – *Perpetual Ideal*
- ☐ Sarah Hilton – *Saltwater Lacuna*
- ☐ Lindsay Miles – *Edeltraut*
- ☐ Blair Trewartha – *Human Energy*
- ☐ Anna Veprinska – *Stone Blossom*
- ☐ Triny Finlay – *Anxious Attachment Style*
- ☐ Alisa Samuel – *Post-Funeral Dance*
- ☐ Darren Bifford – *Some Trivial Reason*
- ☐ Shawn Adrian – *Metanoia's Prairie*
- ☐ Chelsea Coupal – *The Slow Reveal*
- ☐ Margaryta Golovchenko – *Daughterland*

2023

- ☐ Shannon Quinn – *Wonderbeast*
- ☐ Guy Elston – *Automatic Sleep Mode*
- ☐ Sarah Burgoyne – *Air's Error*
- ☐ Emma Rhodes – *Razor Burn*
- ☐ EJ Kneifel – *VIO-LETS*
- ☐ Daze Jefferies – *water/wept*
- ☐ Matt Rader – *Atmospheric Moon River*
- ☐ James Collier – *The Twelve Labours*
- ☐ Melissa Schnarr – *Secondhand Moccasins*
- ☐ Shannon Arntfield – *Fallen Horseman*
- ☐ Marlene Oeffinger – *the night is loud inside my head*
- ☐ Angela Hibbs – *Sky*
- ☐ Christina Shah – *Rig Veda*
- ☐ Janette Platana – *New Fairious*
- ☐ Christopher Patton – *Inanna Scient*
- ☐ Tadhg Saxa – *Seax*
- ☐ derek beaulieu – ☺
- ☐ Y.S. Lee – *Exit Permit*
- ☐ Chris Johnson – *320 lines of poetry*

2024 (January-July)

- ☐ Kirby – *Last Licks*
- ☐ Jason E. Coombs – *Scratching Vinyl Change*
- ☐ Douglas Walbourne-Gough – *Colour Work*
- ☐ Loch Baillie – *Citronella*
- ☐ Jenna Lyn Albert – *mal à l'aise*
- ☐ Ethan Vilu – *Drawings from Before the Red Year*
- ☐ MICHAEL CHANG – *SWEET MOSS*
- ☐ Brian Palmu – *Parade*
- ☐ Sandra Simonds – *Combustible Mood*
- ☐ Margo LaPierre – *In Violet*
- ☐ Jesse Eckerlin – *Almost Nothing*
- ☐ Ayaz Pirani – *Necropolisborough*

Broadsides

☐ Nyla Matuk – "Sails for a Sofa" (2014)
☐ Cassidy McFadzean – "On Wearing the Leggings of Earthy Delights" (2014)
☐ Marc di Saverio – "Evil" (2014)
☐ Jeff Latosik – "The Internet" (2015)
☐ Peter Norman – "What a Window Sees" (2015)
☐ Jordan Scott and Aaron Tucker – "Loss Set 2" (2016)
☐ Kevin Heslop – "Human Beings Have Met to Suture the Wounds" (2020)
☐ David Barrick – "This Sudden Night Walk Holds Everything" (2021)
☐ Klara du Plessis – "Fonds" (2021)
☐ Katie Fewster-Yan – "Gull" (2022)
☐ Shane Neilson – "Be With Us in Our Sadness" (2022)
☐ Michael Prior – "Palinode" (2023)

Manifestos

- ☐ M. Travis Lane – *Truth or Beauty* (2015)
- ☐ Thomas Hodd – *#NoMoreNotes* (2016)
- ☐ John Nyman – *Slogan, Substance, Dream* (2018)
- ☐ John Barton – *Visible but not Seen* (2018)
- ☐ R.M. Vaughn – *Contemporary Art Hates You* (2020)
- ☐ Gregory Betts – *Against Tradition* (2021)
- ☐ Dani Spinosa – *Visual Poetry for Women* (2021)
- ☐ Yusra Usmani – *Poetry as Spectacle* (2023)
- ☐ Robert Colman – *Perfectly Imperfect* (2023)
- ☐ Jay MillAr – *Offline* (2024)

Biographies

Shawn Adrian is a poet from rural Manitoba (Selkirk). He holds a Bachelor of Arts in English with a specialization in creative writing from the University of Winnipeg. His poems have appeared in *Train: a poetry journal*.

Jenna Lyn Albert (they/them | iel) is a genderqueer poet and community organizer living on the traditional unceded and unsurrendered territory of the Wolastoqiyik people. Their debut collection of poetry *Bec & Call* (Nightwood Editions, 2018) won the New Brunswick Book Awards' Fiddlehead Poetry Prize and they served a two-year term as the City of Fredericton's Poet Laureate from 2019-2021. Jenna is currently working on their sophomore collection of poetry and recently published the chapbook *mal à l'aise* with Anstruther Press.

Manahil Bandukwala is the author of *Heliotropia* (Brick Books 2024) and *MONUMENT* (Brick Books 2022). She is the co-creator of Reth aur Reghistan, a multidisciplinary project exploring folklore from Pakistan through poetry, sculpture, and community arts. See her work at manahilbandukwala.com.

Simina Banu is a Canadian poet whose interests are at the intersection of capitalism, technology and mental health. In 2020, she published her debut full-length collection, *POP* (Coach House Books), which won the 2021 ReLit Award for Poetry. She has published several chapbooks: *where art* (words(on)pages), *Tomorrow, adagio* (above/ground press), *harmony in Beach Foam* (Anstruther Press), and *ERE*, a collaboration with Amilcar Nogueira (Collusion Books). In 2024, she released her second full-length poetry collection, *I WILL GET UP OFF OF* (Coach House Books).

David Barrick is the author of *Nightlight* (Palimpsest Press, 2022) as well as the chapbooks *Incubation Chamber* (Anstruther Press, 2019) and *Two Dreams: Stratford and The Copyist* (The Alfred Gustav Press, 2022). His poems appear in *Best Canadian Poetry 2024*, *The Fiddlehead*, *Grain*, *Prairie Fire*, *The Malahat Review*, *THIS Magazine*, and other literary journals. David teaches writing at Western University (London, Ontario).

Gary Barwin is a writer, composer, and multidisciplinary artist. He is the author of many books including *Imagining Imagining: Essays on Language, Identity and Infinity*, *Scandal at the Alphorn Factory: New and Selected Short Fiction 1984-2024*

Biographies

and *Muttertongue* (with Lillian Allen and Gregory Betts). He lives in Hamilton and at garybarwin.com.

Darren Bifford is the author of *Wedding in Fire Country* (Nightwood Editions, 2012) and *False Spring* (Brick Books, 2018). He's published two chapbooks with Anstruther Press: *Age of Revolution* (2017) and *Some Trivial Reason* (2022). He lives in Montreal, where he teaches philosophy.

Alison Braid-Fernandez is the author of the chapbook *Little Hunches* (Anstruther Press, 2020). Her recent work appears in *The Adroit Journal, Massachusetts Review, West Branch,* and *Best Canadian Poetry 2024* and *2025*. She writes and teaches in London, England.

Sarah Burgoyne lives and writes in Montreal. Her books *Because the Sun* (Coach House Books, 2021) and *Saint Twin* (Mansfield Press, 2016) were finalists for the A.M. Klein Prize in Poetry.

MICHAEL CHANG (they/them) is the author of *TOY SOLDIERS* (Action, Spectacle, 2024) & *THINGS A BRIGHT BOY CAN DO* (Coach House Books, 2025). They edit poetry at *Fence*.

Robert Colman is a Newmarket, Ontario-based poet and essayist. His fourth collection of poems, *Ghost Work*, was published with Palimpsest Press in 2024.

Jaclyn Desforges is the queer and neurodivergent author of *Danger Flower* (Anstruther Books), which won the 2022 Hamilton Literary Award for Poetry and was one of CBC's selections for the best Canadian poetry of 2021.

Marc di Saverio is a poet hailing from Hamilton, Ontario. He is the author of *Sanatorium Songs* (Palimpsest Press, 2013), the highly acclaimed epic poem, *Crito di Volta* (Guernica Editions, 2020), and *Songs of My Surrenders* (Guernica Editions, 2023).

Shortlisted for the 2016 bpNichol Chapbook Award, *Wax Lyrical* launched **Klara du Plessis**'s writing career. She has since published five critically-acclaimed books of poetry and non-fiction of which *Ekke* won the 2019 Pat Lowther Memorial

Biographies

Award. *Post-Mortem of the Event* is her most recent collection with Palimpsest Press.

Benjamin C. Dugdale lives and works in rural Alberta (treaty 7 territory). They are the author of *The Repoetic: After Saint-Pol-Roux* (Gordon Hill Press, 2023), and also publish as bonnyCD.

Katie Fewster-Yan is the author of *Surrender and Resistance*. She currently lives in Nova Scotia.

Triny Finlay (she/they) is a queer and genderfluid poet, scholar, teacher, and mother. Their books include *Myself A Paperclip, Histories Haunt Us,* and *Splitting Off.* They live on the unceded and unsurrendered land of Wolastoqiyik, where they teach English and creative writing at the University of New Brunswick.

Patrick Grace is an author and teacher who divides his time between Vancouver and Victoria, BC. He has published two chapbooks: *a blurred wind swirls back for you* (2023), and *Dastardly* (2021), exploring aspects of love, fear, and trauma that represent a personal queer identity. *Deviant* (2024), his first full-length poetry collection, continues to explore these themes, and is available now with University of Alberta Press. He is the managing editor of *Plenitude Magazine*.

Shazia Hafiz Ramji is the author of *Port of Being*, a finalist for the Vancouver Book Award, Dorothy Livesay Poetry Prize (BC Book Prizes), the Gerald Lampert Memorial Award, and recipient of the Robert Kroetsch Award for Innovative Poetry. Her work has recently appeared in *C Mag, CV2,* and the *Literary Review of Canada*. She lives in Toronto, Vancouver, and London, England, where she is at work on a novel.

Angela Hibbs is the author, most recently, of *Control Suppress Delete* (Palimpsest Press, 2017). She lives in Peterborough, Ontario, the traditional territory of the Mississauga First Nations where she teaches elementary school and participates in workshops and radio shows.

Chris Hutchinson is the author of five poetry books as well as the speculative-autobiography-in-verse novel, *Jonas in Frames*. His next poetry collection, *Lost Signal,* is set to be published by Palimpsest Press in 2025.

Biographies

Daze Jefferies (she/her) is an artist, writer, and educator based in Ktaqmkuk (Newfoundland, Canada). She is the author of *water/wept* (Anstruther Press, 2023) and co-author of *Autoethnography and Feminist Theory at the Water's Edge: Unsettled Islands* (Palgrave, 2018). Her work has also been published in *PRISM international, filling Station,* and *Arc Poetry Magazine,* as well as anthologized in *Hustling Verse: An Anthology of Sex Workers' Poetry* (Arsenal Pulp, 2019).

Joseph Kidney won the Short Grain Contest from *Grain* and The Young Buck Poetry Prize from *CV2*. He was published in *Best Canadian Poetry 2024* and nominated for a Canadian National Magazine Award. He is currently completing a PhD in early modern drama at Stanford University. A full-length debut will appear with Goose Lane Editions in 2025.

Kirby's work includes *She* (KFB, 2024); *Last Licks* (Anstruther Press, 2024); *Behold* (2023), a stage adaption of *Poetry is Queer* (Palimpsest Press, 2021); *What Do You Want to Be Called?* (Anstruther Press, 2020) and *This is Where I Get Off* (Permanent Sleep Press, 2019). Their column, "The First Time" is a regular feature at *Send My Love To Anyone.* They are the publisher at knife | fork | book. kirbyshe.com

Virginia Konchan is the author of five books of poetry, *Requiem* (Carnegie Mellon University Press, 2025); *Bel Canto* (Carnegie Mellon, 2022); *Hallelujah Time* (Véhicule Press, 2021); *Any God Will Do* (Carnegie Mellon, 2020); and *The End of Spectacle* (Carnegie Mellon, 2018), as well as a short story collection, *Anatomical Gift*.

Mark Laliberte is a Windsor-based writer/artist/designer whose books include *asemanticasymmetry* (Anstruther Press), *BookBook* (above/ground press), and *Explosive Comic* (Swimmers Group). Laliberte is also a member of MA|DE, a collaborative writing entity, whose debut book of poetry, *ZZOO*, is forthcoming with Palimpsest Press.

M. Travis Lane (born 1934, BA Vassar, PhD Cornell) is a lifetime member of the League of Canadian Poets, a founding member of the Writers' Federation of New Brunswick, and a Raging Granny. She is the author of eighteen books of poetry and prose, and has won numerous awards, among them the Pat Lowther Award,

Biographies

the Alden Nowlan Award, the Bliss Carman Poetry Prize, and the Atlantic Poetry Prize.

R.P. LaRose's poetry has appeared in *PRISM International* and *The Walrus*. His first full-length book, *Wolf Sonnets*, was published in 2022 by Véhicule Press. He resides in amiskwaciy waskahikan (Edmonton).

Allison LaSorda's writing has been nominated for National Magazine Awards and has appeared in *Literary Hub, Brick, The Fiddlehead, Maisonneuve,* and elsewhere. She lives in Halifax.

T. Liem is the author of *Slows: Twice* (Coach House Books, 2023), and *Obits.* (Coach House, 2018), which was shortlisted for a Lambda Literary Award, and won the Gerald Lampert Memorial Award as well as the A.M. Klein Prize. Their writing has been published in *Apogee, Plenitude, The Boston Review, Grain, Maisonneuve, Catapult, The Malahat Review, The Fiddlehead,* and elsewhere. They live in Montreal / Tio'Tia:ke, unceded Kanien'kehá:ka territories.

James Lindsay is author of the poetry collections *Our Inland Sea, Double Self-Portrait, Only Insistence,* and the chapbooks *Ekphrasis! Ekphrasis!, Labour Day,* and *The Lake,* which was nominated for the bpNichol Chapbook Award.

David Ly is the author of *Mythical Man* (2020) and *Dream of Me as Water* (2022), both published under the Anstruther Books imprint of Palimpsest Press, and short-listed for the 2021 and 2023 ReLit Poetry Awards, respectively. He is also co-editor (with Daniel Zomparelli) of *Queer Little Nightmares: An Anthology of Monstrous Fiction and Poetry* (Arsenal Pulp Press, 2022).

Lisa Martin is the author of two full-length collections of poetry, *Believing is not the same as Being Saved* (University of Alberta Press, 2017) and *One crow sorrow* (Brindle & Glass, 2008). Her first novel, *A Story Can Be Told About Pain,* is forthcoming with NeWest Press in spring 2025. She teaches creative writing at MacEwan University in Edmonton.

Terese Mason Pierre (she/her) is a writer whose work has appeared in *The Walrus, ROOM, Brick, Quill & Quire, Uncanny,* and *Fantasy Magazine,* among others. She

Biographies

is an editor at *Augur Magazine* and is the author of two chapbooks. Terese lives and works in Toronto, Canada.

Dr. **Conor Mc Donnell** is an Irish physician and poet. *The Book of Retaliations* (Anstruther Press, 2016) was his first chapbook publication. Since then he has published two other chapbooks (*Safe Spaces, In The Museum*) and two collections of poetry, *Recovery Community* (Mansfield Press, 2021), and *This Insistent List* (ThreadNeedle, 2024). His next collection, *What We Know So Far Is*, will be published in 2025 with Wolsak & Wynn.

Cassidy McFadzean is the author of three books of poetry: *Crying Dress* (House of Anansi Press, 2024), *Drolleries* (McClelland & Stewart, 2019), shortlisted for the Raymond Souster Award, and *Hacker Packer* (M&S, 2015), which won two Saskatchewan Book Awards and was a finalist for the Gerald Lampert Memorial Award. Cassidy was born in Regina, studied poetry at the Iowa Writers' Workshop, and now lives in Toronto.

Amanda Merpaw (she/her) is the author of *Most of All the Wanting* (Palimpsest Press, 2024) and *Put the Ghosts Down Between Us* (Anstruther Press, 2021). Her writing has appeared in a variety of literary journals and with Playwrights Canada Press. She is currently a contributing editor at *Arc Poetry Magazine*.

Khashayar "Kess" Mohammadi is an Iranian-born poet and translator deeply invested in the power of chapbooks and micropress.

Shane Neilson is the Manifesto Series editor at Anstruther Press. RIP Hoppy.

John Nyman is a poet, critic, and book artist from Toronto. His creative works include two poetry collections (*A Devil Every Day* and *Players*), an erasure of words and images from the *Choose Your Own Adventure* series of children's books (*Your Very Own*), and a classic text of Lacanian psycho-analysis reprinted in a nearly illegible typeface (*The Four Fundamental Concepts of Psycho-analysis: A Selection*). John holds a PhD in theory and criticism from Western University and is currently studying to be a lawyer. Find him online at johnnyman.ca

Geographically and professionally peripatetic, **Tolu Oloruntoba**'s careers have included clinical medicine, project management, and poetry. His Anstruther Press

Biographies

chapbook, *Manubrium*, was a bpNichol Chapbook Award finalist. *Manubrium* evolved into his debut full-length collection, *The Junta of Happenstance*, which won the Griffin Poetry Prize and Governor General's Literary Award for Poetry. He lives in Calgary.

Oubah Osman is a writer and poet. She has been published in *20.35 Africa: An Anthology of Contemporary Poetry*, *The New Quarterly*, *The Walrus* and *CV2*, among others. Her chapbook titled *Hereditary Blue* was published by Anstruther Press in 2019, and was shortlisted for the bpNichol Chapbook Award. She is an MFA graduate from the University of Guelph.

Fawn Parker is a Giller-nominated author of five books. Her poetry debut, *Soft Inheritance*, won the Fiddlehead Poetry Book Prize and the J.M. Abraham Atlantic Book Prize. Fawn is currently a PhD candidate at the University of New Brunswick.

Christopher Patton is a poet and literary curator. His visual poetry has appeared in *Diagram*, *Ancient Exchanges*, *Asymptote*, and exhibitions at the Whatcom Museum and the Minnesota Center for Book Arts. His second book of poetry, *Dumuzi*, was published by Gaspereau Press in 2020. He's at work now on a book of poems written in collaboration with an AI named Dragon.

Ayaz Pirani's books include *Happy You Are Here*, *Kabir's Jacket Has a Thousand Pockets*, and *How Beautiful People Are*. He was a resident at Wallace Stegner House and a Scholar at Sewanee Writers' Conference. Ayaz's book of short stories is forthcoming from The Porcupine's Quill.

Janette Platana is the author of the Trillium Award nominated *A Token of My Affliction* (Tightrope, 2015) and the chapbooks *Brother Rat*, *A Queen at 22*, *Lalalazarus*, and *New Fairious*. Her work has been shortlisted for the CBC Literary Award, the Frank O'Connor Award, and the Journey Prize.

Michael Prior's most recent book is *Burning Province* (McClelland & Stewart, 2020), which won the Canada-Japan Literary Prize and the B.C and Yukon Book Prize for Poetry. He edits the Signal Poetry line at Véhicule Press.

Biographies

Jason Purcell is a writer from amiskwacîwâskahikan, Treaty 6 (Edmonton, Alberta). They are the author of *Swollening* (Arsenal Pulp Press) and the chapbook *A Place More Hospitable* (Anstruther Press).

Matt Rader is the author of six collections of poetry, a book of stories, and a work of nonfiction. He lives in Kelowna, BC.

Emma Rhodes (she/her) is a queer writer currently living and working in Tkaronto/Toronto. She is the author of the chapbook *Razor Burn* (Anstruther Press), and the joint chapbook with the Egg Poets Collective *All Things to Keep You Here* (Qwerty Homerow Chapbook Series). Her work has been published in *Contemporary Verse 2, Prism International, Plenitude,* and elsewhere. You can find her at emmarhodes.net.

Melissa Schnarr is Anishinaabe and Kanien'kehá:ka from Bkejwanong Territory (Walpole Island First Nation), with family ties in Six Nations of the Grand River Territory. She is a writer, scholar, and educator who is currently pursuing a PhD in Indigenous education at Western University. She also serves as the chair for Western's Indigenous Writers' Circle and as a visiting artist for the London District Catholic School Board. Her work has appeared in *The Temz Review, TNQ, The Windsor Review, Luna Station Quarterly* and *Yellow Medicine Review*. Her first chapbook, *Secondhand Moccasins,* was published in 2023 by Anstruther Press.

Bardia Sinaee is the author of *Intruder*, which received the Trillium Book Award for Poetry. He was the guest editor of *Best Canadian Poetry 2024*. He was born in Tehran, Iran, and currently lives in Ottawa.

Emily Skov-Nielsen is the author of *The Knowing Animals* (Brick Books). She has worked for *The Fiddlehead* and *Studies in Canadian Literature* and is now a librarian. She lives in New Brunswick, at the end of a river, with her family.

Mahaila Smith (any pronouns) is a young femme writer, living and working on the traditional territory of the Algonquin Anishinabeg in Ottawa, Ontario. They are one of the co-editors for *The Sprawl Mag*. Their debut chapbook, *Claw Machine*, was published by Anstruther Press in 2020. Their second chapbook, *Water-Kin* was published by Metatron Press in 2024. Their novelette in verse, *Seed Beetle*, is forthcoming with Stelliform Press.

Biographies

Dani Spinosa is a poet of digital and print media, a software developer, and a flavoured coffee enthusiast. She has published several chapbooks of poetry, several more peer-reviewed journal articles on poetry, one long scholarly book, and one pink poetry book.

Blair Trewartha's debut poetry collection, *Easy Fix* (Palimpsest Press, 2014), was shortlisted for the Relit Award. He is the author of three chapbooks: *Break In* (Cactus Press, 2010), *Porcupine Burning* (Baseline Press, 2012), and *Human Energy* (Anstruther Press, 2022). His recent publications include *The Dalhousie Review*, *Prairie Fire Magazine*, and *The Fiddlehead*, and his second full-length book is forthcoming with Palimpsest Press in 2026.

Yusra Usmani is a writer and poet whose non-fiction explores the role of literature in religion, and she frequently employs religious and alchemic symbolism in her poetry. Some relevant publications include *The Cattle* with Bottlecap Press and *Al-Hashashin* with The Blasted Tree.

Douglas Walbourne-Gough is a poet and mixed/adopted status member of the Qalipu Mi'kmaq First Nation from Elmastukwek (the Bay of Islands), Ktaqmkuk (Newfoundland). His first collection, *Crow Gulch*, won the 2021 EJ Pratt Poetry Award. His second collection, *Island*, centres around the Newfoundland Mi'kmaq experience in the wake of the Qalipu enrolment process and is forthcoming in fall 2024, also from Goose Lane Editions. He holds an MFA in creative writing (UBC Okanagan) and a PhD in English/creative writing (UNB Fredericton).

Matthew Walsh is a poet from the Maritimes whose two collections, *These Are Not the Potatoes of my Youth* (2019) and *Terrarium* (2024), were published by Icehouse/Goose Lane Editions. They have also published short stories on *Joyland* and *The Capra Review*.

Lily Wang's debut novel, *Silver Repetition*, was published in February 2024 by House of Anansi Press. They are also the poet of *Saturn Peach* (Gordon Hill Press, 2018).

About the Editor

Jim Johnstone is a Toronto-based poet, editor, and critic. He is the author of seven books of poetry, most recently *The King of Terrors* (Coach House Books, 2023), and a collection of essays on micropress: *Write, Print, Fold, and Staple* (Gaspereau Press, 2023). Along with his wife, Erica Smith, he is the publisher at Anstruther Press, which is the subject of *The Anstruther Reader: Ten Years of Poems, Broadsides, and Manifestos* (Palimpsest Press, 2024).

Printed by Imprimerie Gauvin
Gatineau, Québec